CW00431212

Are You Sure
That's What You Saw?

A collection of encounters

with the paranormal

Copyright © October 2020 Kate Fromings

Edited by Lynne Fromings

All rights reserved.

ISBN: 9798616445285

CONTRIBUTORS

(Here are the people who agreed to be named.
Others have been provided with a pseudonym to
protect their identity)

Kate Fromings

Chris Barrie

Kirstie Burroughs

Nathaniel Merryweather

N.M. Rowley

Alex Barrett

Lynne F

CONTENTS

INTRODUCTION

You may have noticed that there is no author mentioned on the front cover of this book. I made this decision as I felt it would be wrong to take sole credit for what you are about to read. Of course, I have a couple of personal experiences which I documented, but this collection isn't about me.

It's about all the people that felt they had a strange story to tell. It's about people that were too embarrassed to mention these encounters to their friends or family for fear of ridicule. It's about documenting real incidents that remain, to this day, unexplained.

The accounts you are about to read were gathered from members of the public in various locations around Britain. Some take place as far back as the 1960s, other are only a few years old. Each person that had the courage to come forward has assisted in creating a piece of history that will inform and intrigue readers both currently, and in the future.

'Paranormal' is defined by the internationally respected Collins Dictionary as: *"A paranormal event or power, for example the appearance of a ghost, it cannot be explained by scientific laws and is thought to involve strange, unknown forces."*

Within this book you will find instances of suspected ghosts, UFOs and unknown phenomena. Due to some subject matter it is advised that you are aged 18+ when reading this novel.

— Kate Fromings, Author

The Maid And The Soldier

Anastasia K

I know most people say they can't remember much before they were about eight years old, but I swear I remember this from when I was around five. I can also remember snatches of stuff from my fourth birthday, and a holiday I went on to Disneyland when I was six... I just think that some things stay with you - especially if they are different from your everyday life.

My family's from a village near Stockport, and my cousins live in this other villagey kind of area on the outskirts of Manchester. My own home was a council flat, built in the seventies. We didn't have a garden or a balcony, so I always loved visiting other family members. The best trips were when I had the chance to sleep over.

Being an only child, my parents often packed me off to my gran or my aunt closer to Stockport. For some reason, on the night in question, I was having to go to my dad's sister's house for a 'surprise' sleep over. I guess it was early winter as I hadn't had my dinner and it was already dark outside.

Mum drove me over. She dropped me off and quickly left. My aunt and uncle seemed a bit annoyed that I was there. They put all my overnight things in my cousin Jennifer's room, and said I'd be sleeping on the floor next to her bed. I was dazed by all the sudden commotion, but excitement soon took over... I remember we all ate pizza and chips in front of the telly before going to bed.

My cousins' house was really old. When I checked on the Internet with Google Street View, it looks Victorian, or at least turn of the twentieth century. It was also *really* cold and draughty. They didn't have carpets; it was all waxed wooden floorboards and the occasional rug. Most of the other houses in the row had been turned into studio apartments. I was used to having just the one level to live on, with our neighbours one storey above us. My auntie and uncle had three floors in their home, and a room at the very top which we called the 'attic room'.

When it came time for bed, Jennifer and I were so excited and hyper that my aunt began to get irritated with us. She told us off for messing around, making us promise to be quiet because Jennifer's room had no door. Everyone downstairs would hear us, even if we walked around on tiptoe. I remember we hid under our bedding, and when she had gone Jennifer produced some sweets, which we hurriedly ate, trying not to laugh too loudly.

Anyway, a couple of hours passed and I heard the rest of the household go to bed. The lights were turned off. What I could make out from my position on the floor was a perfectly framed image of the landing through the open doorway. I could see the top of the winding wooden stairs that led down from the tiny square piece of floor in front of the bedroom. There was a roof window, with no curtain, above the stairs which lit up the whole scene with silvery moonlight. The bottom of the stairwell was now so dark I couldn't even make out the walls, but everything else was clear as day.

I closed my eyes and tried to get to sleep. After all the sugar and the laughing I started to feel sick... and I missed my parents.

I called out for my aunt and she reluctantly came upstairs, telling me to go to sleep. After she left I just couldn't settle. I was wrapped in my single duvet, the floor was hard and I really wasn't feeling well. I called out again, this time my uncle came upstairs. He had work the next day and told me off for shouting. He said it would be morning soon, and the quicker I went to sleep the faster I could get up and go back home. I was pretty upset by this point, but I didn't want to cry. All the while Jennifer was lying in her nice warm bed, and I could hear her constant breathing.

I was worried that my aunt and uncle would tell my parents I was being awkward, so I tried to close my eyes and think about nice things like the pizza and fun we had had earlier on.

From what I remember, I did get to sleep for a little bit, when I opened my eyes it was still dark outside and I really needed the bathroom. I was a bit frightened of going down the narrow staircase into the dark, but I knew if I turned on the light Jennifer would wake up and make a fuss. I held off as long as I could, and finally got the courage to make the short dash downstairs.

It's important that you realise I was wide awake at this point, sitting up with my duvet wrapped around me like a shawl. I had been awake for quite some time. I was just about to stand up when I saw someone's head and shoulders coming up the stairs. I froze thinking it was a family member who'd heard me wriggling around on the creaky floorboards. It became clear very quickly that I didn't know this person, and there was somebody else with them too...

I wasn't scared by what I saw I was just really, really confused. A man with dark brown hair in a red soldier's uniform, with cream coloured trousers, was walking up the stairs. I could see the detail on his jacket, the dirt on his trouser legs... He stopped on the landing no more than a couple of metres from where I was sitting in the room.

Then, coming up straight after him, was a short woman wearing the black and white uniform of a housemaid. She had long blonde hair and a small white bonnet on her head. The only way I could describe it was like watching a film or a TV show being projected in thin air, but the people weren't transparent.

I watched them for what seemed like ages, it was probably only thirty seconds. They embraced on the landing, they both smiled at each other and then the maid started to go back down the stairs. At this moment both of them disappeared immediately, like someone had turned off the film. I think that's what actually scared me. There were also no footsteps, no sounds at all.

I started to cry and I called out for my uncle. He came running up the stairs again, more frazzled than the last time, and told me I was having a bad dream. He took me to the bathroom and then gave me an extra blanket to lie on. Jennifer swears she didn't wake up through all of this, so I am the only one who saw the couple. I know I wasn't asleep because I had been awake so long, deciding how I was going to get to the bathroom - I felt cold and had a cramp in my leg, which was keeping me alert.

The only things I have been able to find out about the house was that the attic room was the original servant's quarters, and there was a large military base at Ardwick Green so it's possible soldiers would have been in the area when the house was built.

The part that doesn't match up is that the soldier's cream trousers seemed to be from the time of the Napoleonic war, seventy years before the army base was even functioning. Either way, it was really strange and I've never experienced anything similar since.

Footsteps

Chris B

I used to work over in the Southside of Glasgow, in a nursery school in Busby. I was the supervisor of after-school care. As such, I was often the last one left in the building when the kids went home - this was the best opportunity to catch up on my paperwork without being distracted.

One night everyone went home as usual, leaving me to get on with the million and one things on my list. I was pretty engrossed, and I wanted to get finished before the chaos that came when the cleaners began. They had to move the furniture around to vacuum and sweep under everything.

It was a cold dark winter's evening, and the room I was using was barely lit, as most of the lights in that part of the building had been switched off. It left me with just enough illumination to work by without straining my eyes. The shutters on the outside of the windows had already been closed, so the car park floodlights didn't even penetrate the room.

The lack of light ensured the room maintained an atmospheric murky quality; anything outside of my desk was essentially just a shadow. A loose shutter banging in the wind periodically broke the still silence, the quiet aftermath of thirty noisy small children. There was nothing unusual about that as the building was quite old.

After fifteen minutes or so I heard the outer door

open. Heavy footsteps walked down the hallway by me. The lights remained off, but I didn't give a thought to that, as I was too focussed on my paperwork. The classroom door wasn't flush to the floor, so anyone turning the light on in the hall would have caused a large strip of yellow light on the carpet. I just assumed that the person was busy, and would turn the lights on at my end when they came back that way.

Moments later I shouted out to the cleaners, Ian and Elizabeth, that I was almost finished. I joked that I would get out of their way soon... but oddly, I didn't get a response. Unperturbed by this I carried on with my work. After all, they could have been listening to music through their headphones and not heard me. The corridor was long enough for three classrooms either side so, just as before, they could have been working up at the far end.

About five minutes after that I finally finished and got up to leave. I walked down the gloomy hallway towards the exit. I heard the external door open, as it had before. The main light came on immediately and in walked Ian and Elizabeth with their outdoor coats on!

This puzzled me because at least one of them *must* have come in earlier, as I heard the footsteps and the door open. That could only have been done by someone with the master key - me, or them. So I asked if either had been in earlier. They both looked at each other in confusion, and then back to me. In unison they explained that, no, they had only just arrived to start their shift.

A chill ran down my spine and I was a little creeped out. At the time I calmed myself down by thinking that one of the teaching staff must have come back for something they had forgotten, like a text book or a bag. The footsteps had sounded heavy and deliberate though, not rushed and light...

The next day I asked all the staff and nobody admitted to being responsible for the phantom footsteps. Everyone, even the secretary, had left me alone in the small building to finish my work in peace... that's when I realised this was weird. I wasn't scared at the time I heard the footsteps, so I know my mind wasn't playing tricks on me. I wasn't panicking. It's just something I can't explain away.

Plague Grave

Simon S

We went on a mini road trip. It was just me and a couple of friends, I was driving. We had heard that near Devilla Forest there was another bit of woods closer to the river, where there was a couple of big stones. These were locally known as a kid's plague grave from hundreds of years ago.

We looked up some stuff on the Internet and found out where to park. It was really muddy and down this track which looked like it went nowhere. When I parked up there was a handpainted sign, like someone had just rushed it off, and it pointed down a thin footpath saying 'plague grave'.

The footpath was between a wire fence on the right and an old stone wall on the left marking the border of the wooded bit. Me and the others came to a stile and climbed over; but the main footpath carried on straight, heading towards the big power station opposite Grangemouth.

Once we were over the stile it was hard to see the track through the fallen leaves. One of my mates was a DJ and he had brought with him a Tascam audio recorder to see if we could get any spooky voices. It was all a bit of a joke. It was autumn time and the guys kept chucking piles of leaves at each other, then two of them got pissed off and decided to go back to the car. It left me, John and my friend Andy trying to find these big grey stones in the wood.

Eventually we did find them, and they weren't that big, but people had tied little bits of material on bushes around the grave and there were some fake plastic flowers on it. There wasn't any words engraved on it, just some big flat stones laid down, like about four foot by two foot.

It wasn't raining, but it was getting cold because it was the afternoon. On the website some local history people had said that these kids used to live on a farm. Then when the Black Death came up to Scotland they died and the farmer couldn't bury them in a church, so he buried them there on his land, and since then the trees have grown up into the woods.

It didn't feel spooky. John and Andy kept mucking about and making 'whoooo' ghost noises. Anyway, after a while they got bored and Andy put down his sound recorder on the top of the gravestones. It's not connected to the Internet or anything. It's just a digital sound recorder, like one of those old Dictaphones that used to use tapes.

Him and John started asking questions like "Is there anybody here?" and "If you are the dead children give us a sign". Of course, nothing happened but they continued asking and leaving gaps in case anything came out in the audio when we listened to it back.

I suddenly noticed that it felt a bit weird and I couldn't work out why. Then I realised it was because there were no bird or nature noises; just the trees moving a little bit. At this point the battery warning sign came up on the recorder and the other two said they wanted to go and get more double As from the car.

I said I'd wait at the grave and the recording could continue.

So, I thought it would be interesting to video the recorder on the grave so that if anything happened I could prove it wasn't being knocked around and no twigs or anything were touching it or scraping it. I turned my phone on airplane mode to make sure no signals interfered with the recorder or anything.

I put my phone down and then I sat down too so I wasn't moving about. I clapped my hands a couple of times to synch up the audio and video later. The others didn't come back for ages and then the Tascam recorder ran out of battery. When I turned my phone back on they had messaged me saying they couldn't be bothered to walk back, and to meet them back at the car.

I was a bit pissed off, so I got the recorder and walked back through the woody bit. The birds and stuff only started again when I was over the stile and back on the narrow track walking back to the car. When I got back there they were passing round a joint and looking at their phones. They weren't even bothered and didn't ask if anything happened, so I just kept the recorder in my pocket and drove us all back to our home town about forty minutes away.

Anyway, fast forward like two weeks and I find the recorder in my jeans pocket when I'm getting dirty clothes sorted for the wash. I decided to listen to it back using the soundbar speakers in my living room. The first thing I notice is that there are loads of bird noises on it - which I never heard at the time.

I think 'that must have a really sensitive microphone'. But when you hear John and Andy messing around and asking questions they sound quiet, not like it was super amped up. So then I hear my claps and I think 'oh yeah I still have the video on my phone'. I get my phone and synch up the video with the audio recorder.

I'm looking at my phone screen listening to the soundbar. Nothing's happening on the video, just like the odd dry leaf moving on the ground in the background. Then on the audio there's this weird noise that makes me jump. It's a digital glitch noise. Like something you'd put in a kids cartoon or a film when you want a glitch sound effect, really electronic. Nothing in the video shows anything touching the Tascam recorder. Then, a minute later, the same type of noise but slightly different in length.

After that I stopped the playback and checked my video with its own phone sound at the same points, and it's not on the video, just the audio recording. So I play back the audio and turn it up, using a couple of basic music EQs to see if I can hear what it is, but it just sounds like a glitch, like a digital artefact or something.

It was a bit weird but, because I didn't know what it was and I hadn't felt creeped out at the time, I just assumed it was something where the recorder had glitched. I messaged one of Andy's friends - who is a professional sound engineer for a well-known music equipment company - and asked if there was any way he could take the audio file and run it through some filters to see if anything came up.

He was really sceptical and was saying things like

"ghosts don't exist" and "it will just be some bad soldering inside the recorder or a loose connection that caused it." Next time we met up I gave him the SD card with the direct file on it, not expecting to hear anything back apart from getting laughed at.

A couple of days after that I got a weird text message on my phone. It just said,

"Do you want your SD card back?" So I was like,

"Of course I do, it's sixteen gig LOL. Did you manage to hear anything else or were they just glitches?" Straight away the audio guy replies,

"I don't want to talk about it mate."

At this point I'm pretty confused, he hasn't said 'no' and he hasn't told me what he found. So I asked him again and this time he rings me back and his voice sounds really stressed. He basically said that he messed around with the whole recording, running it through filters, compressors and slowing it down and stuff. Then when it hit the two glitches, he knew straight away this wasn't normal digital artefacts on an MP3 or electronic interference.

Obviously, I wanted to know what it was or what could have caused it. This guy, I swear down, he told me to leave it alone and that he never wants to hear that track again. I kept trying to joke like 'It's only fifteen minutes long, I'll pay you twenty quid' and the guy said I couldn't pay him a hundred to listen to that again and that he didn't even want the SD card in his studio.

So, I honestly don't know what was on that recording as I never got the SD card back. It ended up getting thrown away. All I know is that I didn't hear birds in the wood but they showed up on the recording, and whatever was in those couple of seconds of 'glitches' scared a fifty year old man who doesn't believe in ghosts.

Notch In The Clouds

Alex H

So this was a summer, on the weekend. The sun was out. There were cumulus type chunky, white clouds. I was in the garden, hanging out the washing - this was when I lived at my mum and dad's house in Kent. Something just glinted in the sky across from me and I looked up.

It was like a bullet shape; it had a flat end and then at the other bit it was a sort of pointy end. It had a kind of cigar shape. It wasn't full-on pointed like an arrow; the end was rounded off a bit. The thing looked quite small because it was up at cloud height, but I could tell it was chrome coloured. That's what had reflected the sunlight when it glinted at me. It was definitely shiny. When I was looking up it literally moved *through* the cloud.

It cut a section of the cloud away. It cut it out, like a notch. I love aircraft and I was studying physics at the time in order to start a career in the RAF, so I was quite surprised when I saw it just 'remove' the thick cloud. I hadn't seen anything in videos of similar aircraft or read about any in development that had that characteristic.

So, after it had cut through the cloud, it disappeared. It didn't zoom off at high speed, it didn't fly off or change direction away from me - it disappeared. It wasn't there anymore. I was like 'that's really odd'.

Then, just as I happened to witness all of that, my dad came out into the garden for a cigarette. I said,

"Dad, can you see that weird gap in the cloud?" I didn't tell him what I had just seen that had created it though. He looked where I was pointing and straight away said,

"What? That missing bit there? That's a bit odd." He could see the gap too, the point being it wasn't something I was imagining or hallucinating. I hadn't made it up; he could definitely see it and stood looking at the sky for a while.

When he had finished looking he dismissed it as a way the clouds must have formed from air currents or thermals up there. I didn't correct him. I just agreed and continued hanging out the washing. However, around the same time that I saw the strange aircraft, I also started experiencing a strange coincidence.

That same day, in the evening, I looked at the clock and it was 23:11. When I look back and think about it, the time that I would have seen the UFO was around 11:11 in the morning. For the next month or so every time I looked at my watch, a computer screen, my mobile phone (pre smart phones), or a public clock like at a train station - it was always 11:11.

You could surmise that I was looking out for this and so, subconsciously, I was checking the time on devices around eleven o'clock - but I wasn't. There were instances where I had no control over the time, such as educational exams. If an exam was due to finish at, say, twelve, and I finished writing early I would then pick up my old-style mobile phone from the front desk and turn it on... at 11:11.

Another example was my watch battery running out, and when I turned on my PC to get the correct time from the Internet it was 11:11. After several weeks of this happening it suddenly stopped, and I can honestly say it has never started again.

I don't know what I saw that day, I have tried to look up other UFO sightings and there are some in the USA that match what I described above, yet none of them are exactly the same. In all honesty, it could have been a new craft that the military were trying out, but there are lots of little air fields near my parent's house and it's on a flight path to and from Gatwick Airport, as well as having the air ambulance helicopter site nearby - so why would they test it there?

The military wouldn't be carrying out test flights in such a busy area, over a densely populated part of the county.

The Haunted Vestry

Joanne L

I'm from in a small village in Oxfordshire, I've always lived here and I know the community pretty well. I've never heard of anyone else telling a similar story, and I didn't have any preconceived ideas about what to expect all those years ago... which is why I believe I saw a ghost.

My father was the choir master of our local church. It's a really old, traditional building - it's often featured on postcards of the area because it's so picturesque, with its belfry and well-kept graveyard. There were only a few choir members at the time this happened - probably less than fifteen. Most of the choir was made up of old people who had always sung at the church, and a few kids whose parents wanted them to keep out of trouble on a Friday night.

I was about eleven when the incident took place. One night in November we finished our regular practise for the carol concert, the other kids had already been picked up from the churchyard gates. The organist had gone home, and the last couple of old people were having a chat by the large main door of the church.

It was a traditional grey sandstone stone set up, with wooden pews and pretty stained glass windows. It was a wide, open space; the only parts that were not part of the main church space were the vestry at the back of the seating area and, at the opposite end, a small chapel to the right of the altar.

Each of the above mentioned parts was separated from the main church by ornate dark carved mahogany screens with intricate designs of foliage and angel's faces. The one by the little chapel area had arched window openings so, although it was a closed off, you could easily see into it. The chapel also had its own small arched wooden door that I always used with my dad when leaving the church after choir practise.

The old women finally finished talking and hobbled off, out of the main church door, closing it behind them. The main door marked the halfway point of the church, between the vestry and the chapel, with rows and rows of dark wooden pews filling in the seating area. If you don't know what a vestry is, it's the large room where the choir and the vicar get changed into their robes when they are performing a service. Our one also had a conference table in it for parish meetings.

The vestry was located directly below the metal organ pipes. It was also the only access to the bell tower. The decorated wooden screen that closed it off from the main part of the church was almost as high as the organ pipes, and there was a set of double doors with clear glass panels in them. The panels were made in an antique style with diamond shaped leaded lights. You could still make out people in the room, so a heavy blue velvet curtain had been hung inside the vestry to protect people's privacy.

If you think of any classic design of a church in the south of England, cold stone floors, hard pews, the smell of beeswax polish, tattered hymn books laid out for the Sunday service... you wouldn't be far off this one.

It was a Friday night, and it's important to note that the bell tower was locked (the ringers had their rehearsals on a Wednesday). The vicar didn't attend choir practises either, so it was just me and my dad left in the empty church. After every session ended, he would ask me to collect the books and sheet music and return them to the vestry. While I tidied up, he locked the lid of the piano and did his rounds to make sure everyone had left the church, before systematically locking the external main door and turning off the lights.

This was in the nineties and, being a close-knit Christian community, there was no need for alarms or security cameras. Everything that needed to be secured away was within thick wooden chests with iron catches. Even the main door to the church wasn't alarmed, as it was so old and heavy that once it was bolted it would take a good few healthy men to attempt a break in!

So, while my dad checked the building for people, I scooped up all the music and carried it up the main aisle of the church towards the vestry. My footsteps echoed off the hard walls, and among my own echoes I heard my dad clicking locks and turning keys. At this point the lights were all on, apart from in the dark vestry ahead of me.

Because I knew where to put the books I didn't bother turning on the main light, I just walked in and placed them on the usual shelves. There was a clear leaded window at one end behind the conference table and with the street light outside by the wall of the graveyard, that was enough to illuminate the room.

I checked the bell tower door was still locked, and

then as I left the room, I closed the blue velvet curtain. I shut the double wooden glass doors. The small iron key was already in place so I turned the lock and pulled on them to make sure they were fully closed. They were.

All I could see was the darkness of the blue curtain fabric and my face reflected in the small diamond-shaped panes of glass.

I took the key and joined my dad in the centre of the church. I remember we had some conversation about the bats living in the roof... He took the vestry key from me and told me to go and wait in the small chapel while he did one last check and turned off all the lights.

I did as I was told but I didn't wait within the chapel behind the wooden screen. I stood outside it, leaning against it, watching my dad walk back up the main aisle of the church. Our church has two aisles; they form the shape of a cross. The main aisle, the vertical one, has the vestry at one end, and the altar and choir stalls at the other.

The second aisle, the horizontal one, runs from the main door of the church to a bulletin board on the far wall. This whole area is open with only empty, low, wooden pews in rows - there's nowhere for anyone to hide. When my dad reached the intersection he decided not to check the vestry and just went left, to the electric power switches by the main door. I was getting bored by this point and wondering what was on TV, so I let my mind wander... The lights started going off, one section of pews at a time. First the choir and altar section, then the congregation area, until only the light by the chapel area was left on (this had its own switch by the little arched doorway).

As my dad started to walk back towards me I noticed that something wasn't right. Behind him, I saw one of the double doors to the vestry open.

My first feeling was annoyance as I assumed I had not locked it properly. But then I realised that the heavy blue curtain wasn't pulled fully across, and there was a black opening. A space had been made for someone to walk through the doorway and straight into the room. I was about to call out to my dad, who was ten metres away from me. Then I saw a figure dressed in white robes, with a light green stole, go into the vestry from the back pews of the main church!

There was no noise, and the person couldn't have been hiding in the pews, especially in full Anglican robes. I couldn't see the person's face because the only muted light was coming in from the stained glass windows in the main church. It was enough to make out shapes and even the pattern on the carpet, but the figure was just too far away to catch a glimpse of its face.

I assumed it was our vicar as the body shape seemed to be the same, and I recognised the outfit.

I wasn't scared.

I called out to my dad and pointed at the back of the church. I told him someone was still in there and he turned around. By the time he had turned on his heels and taken a couple of steps back, I realised that the vestry doors were both shut as I had left them... and the blue curtain was still pulled across...

My dad checked the doors and confirmed they were both locked. He said I must have imagined it. As he came back to where I was waiting at the chapel, I kept looking at the vestry... but nothing more happened. I felt a bit uneasy, as it wasn't as if I had turned my head and seen something in my peripheral vision. It was the full figure of a vicar and it had moved. I must have watched the whole thing for about twenty seconds.

Anyway, my dad unlocked the side door of the chapel and I waited outside while he turned off the last light and locked the little door behind us. I kept telling him, *I was adamant*, I had seen someone. Reluctantly he said we should walk around the perimeter of the building and look through all the windows to settle my mind.

We started walking around the back of the chapel, we passed the end of the church (where inside there was the altar and choir stalls). Then there was a section with no stained glass windows (this was where the piano was and also the bulletin board inside).Then we walked a bit further and came to the bottom of the bell tower, and finally we walked around the last corner to the end where the vestry was.

We were walking past the external vestry wall, when I thought I heard a man's voice, muffled inside. It was as if someone was in there speaking. But the stone walls were so thick, there was no way you could hear a single person's voice on the outside, not to mention some of the walls were lined with the cupboards full of robes and flags. I continued to chat to my dad about any old nonsense just to take my mind off it.

We turned the last corner and walked under the clear large leaded window... we could see the street light and moonlight landing on the conference table inside. Although the glass was warped and wobbly, it was obvious that nobody was in the room. I could even make out the white lining on the back of the blue curtain that I had pulled across the door earlier.

Satisfied, we walked to the churchyard gate that led onto the quiet main road of the village. Before we crossed over to walk home, I looked back at the vestry window. To my surprise, I saw the perfect outline of the same figure I had seen in the church, standing by the window!

It looked as if it was facing the road watching me and dad leave!

I tugged on my dad's coat sleeve and he asked what I wanted, but by the time I opened my mouth to say 'turn around' the figure had vanished.

Looking back on that memory, you could say - at a stretch - that the blue curtain had for some reason twisted itself around and what I saw at a distance when I was inside the church was just the curtain flapping around in the vestry. But that wasn't possible. The curtain was so heavy that it took a great effort to draw it across on the thick brass pole and sometimes it needed two people to do it... besides that, I don't know how to explain the white-clad figure at the vestry window as that is the opposite end of the room to the door curtain and the internal doors.

I have never heard anyone else speak about the church being haunted, not even the graveyard has any ghost stories. To this day I still believe I saw the spirit of a former clergyman.

Blue Boots

Daniel C

When I was a kid, I used to spend most of the school summer holidays at my grandparent's house in central London. It was a town house in the middle of a terrace, with a massive back garden. It was in a row of Victorian houses that had once been quite posh but, by the time I knew them in the nineties, they had been turned into flats and bedsits... all except my grandparents'.

The houses back onto a hill, and this is important for my story. If you walk up the front steps to the ground floor front door, this is level of the house with the back yard and patio area. Then when you walk through the ground floor rooms, out onto the courtyard patio, ahead of you is a steep double-width flight of grey stone steps. These lead up to the lawn and flowerbeds. All of the garden is on a terraced slope leading away from the house towards the top of the hill.

Mine and my brother's temporary bedroom was on the ground floor. We called it the 'garden room' as it had a large glass door that led directly out onto the paved courtyard patio area at the bottom of the steps. In the heat of the August afternoons we would usually choose to go to our bedroom and read books rather than get scorched outside. The whole garden was like a giant suntrap, so going inside and leaving the sliding door open was a welcome break from the heat.

At the time the incident happened, I was about ten and my brother was eight. We had separate single beds facing the glass door, and we were both laying down on our fronts reading books. From what I can remember, I was reading a book about the countryside and my brother was reading a funny story by Roald Dahl. This is significant, we weren't the kind of kids to scare each other or read spooky stories.

So, it's the middle of the day. For some reason I look up from my book, out of the door, towards the patio courtyard. We can barely see the top of the flight of steps from our room. It's just a slither, a few inches where you can see a band of green as the steps finish and the lawn starts. Suddenly, along the top of the steps at the edge of the lawn, I see two feet walking casually from one side to the other. It was as if they had come out of the first floor back door of the house.

I didn't think anything of it. I assumed it was my granny.

I carried on looking for another few seconds and I realised that the shoes the person was wearing looked strange... they were pale blue ankle boots with a slight heel, and what looked like a couple of black buttons on the side. They didn't just look strange, they looked like something you'd see in a museum. I turned to speak to my brother. He was already staring at the same place as me, with a weird look on his face.

When I looked back to the top of the steps the boots were still there. I could also see the hem of a pale blue dress with a white bit of petticoat showing. The person was walking backwards and forwards slowly, as if they were waiting for someone to join them. Then, without warning the boots, everything, disappeared! My brother started to whimper and get afraid so I told him not to worry and that it was probably just Granny.

At that moment, there was a knock on our bedroom door and it really *was* Granny asking if we wanted anything to drink. We looked at each other, both knowing that there was no way she could have got from the top of the garden steps to our internal bedroom door by going through the house in such a short amount of time... When we opened the bedroom door she was wearing a pale pink T-shirt and white capri-style trousers. On her feet she had gold open-toed sandals; no sign of boots or a skirt.

I tried to talk about this with my brother that night but, being younger than me, I think he was scared and just wanted to ignore it. When I've brought it up as an adult he apparently doesn't remember any of it, but I know what I saw.

Anyway, fast forward a few years and I'm a teenager. I was still too young to stay at home all day and look after my brother, so we were spending another summer at my grandparents'. This time, again, it was midday and we were all sitting on deck chairs on the edge of the lawn at the top of the steps. From there we could look back at the house and see down into the courtyard patio area.

As far as we were aware, everyone in the house at the time was sitting outside; me, my brother, my granny and my grandad. We were discussing something to do with a board game we had been playing. For some reason I looked back at the house to the dining room window. It was directly opposite me on the first floor, about twenty metres away.

Sitting there, looking out of the window, was a young woman with blonde hair. She looked upset and was staring straight at us. She had a kind of bluish-white dress on but I couldn't tell (due to the reflection on the glass) what style it was. I knew she was in the room. She wasn't a 'reflection' herself on the outside of the window, because the sunlight on the glass was in front of her face and torso. Everything about her had a violet hue.

I looked back to my grandparents to see if they had seen her, but they were deep in conversation. This time I decided to confront them and tell them what I had seen. They dismissed it as one of our older cousins (both of whom had blonde hair) in the house. They had a set of keys, coming and going freely every day.

As soon as my grandad finished saying that, both my cousins *did* appear... but from the courtyard door at the *bottom* of the steps. Both of them were wearing dark clothes. They had their hair neatly tied back in a modern style. They looked nothing like the person I had seen at the window.

We asked them if they'd been in the dining room, or upstairs, and they told us they hadn't. They'd just come in through the bottom of the house, they didn't have any need to go upstairs. Just like the blue boots from my childhood, I knew the person I had seen at the window couldn't be explained away.

Years later when I was a young adult, I asked my grandad about the history of the house. He told me that one family lived there from the moment it was built in the late Victorian era. My grandparents had bought it in the nineteen-fifties after the last remaining spinster granddaughter from that original family had passed away.

Apparently, it was common knowledge that she never married because she was waiting for her soldier to come home from the First World War. He never returned.

I don't know if the boots belonged to the person I saw sitting in the dining room but, either way, I always have an odd feeling when I visit their house, especially if I am left alone in any of the top rooms.

Night Visitors

Nathaniel Merryweather

A little background to the following tale first.

When I was about three years old I started receiving 'night visitors'. They only appeared when I was alone, and they looked like small frenetic spinning discs, about the size of marbles, in the corner of my bedroom.

At first one, then two, they would manifest sometimes as my mum, sometimes as my dad. They would approach my bed and I would start screaming the house down! If one appeared as my mum, then my real mum came in it would make me worse, and my dad would have to come and attend to me instead.

I now know that these 'discs' are called orbs, and that the manifestations I had seen were shape-shifters. One time my toy panda stood up at the end of my bed, walked towards me and put its paws around my neck. In these situations my parents always told me that I was 'having a bad dream' and to 'go back to sleep'. The thing is... I hadn't ever been asleep. It's frustrating when you aren't believed, nor taken seriously.

By the age of sixteen I had turned to the Christian church for answers - which I didn't receive. Eventually, at the age of twenty-three, I turned to the practise of Wicca - which did start to give me the answers I needed. Amongst other things, I learned about psychic protection. However, Wicca also made me more vulnerable as I was learning a lot about the manipulation of energy. This is known to attract the attention of dark entities, which take advantage of the inexperienced.

The first attack came three weeks before the main events.

I had just fallen asleep when I awoke in a state of paralysis and awareness. I didn't know what was occurring, but something was trying to drag me out of my bed. I struggled for many minutes before I was able to sit up and make it stop. There was no change of consciousness, I didn't suddenly 'wake up'. I had been alert the whole time. I thought it was strange, but I went back to sleep. It happened again, stronger, and longer - it was terrifying. It was not a dream.

After about three weeks I had pushed the incident to the back of my mind and kind of forgotten about it. This next time it was different. I felt like I was at the bottom of a deep pit. It was dark. I could hear screaming. I struggled up until I could finally open my eyes. My girlfriend, in bed with me, was the one screaming.

She was saying over and over "The eyes! The eyes!" I got her calmed down and asked what was wrong. She told me that she had awoken to a feeling that there was someone else in the room, and a foul smell. She said it was as though a dead body had been dragged off a compost heap and set fire to. She had then turned to wake me up and was confronted by two of me.

There was me lying in bed and, about a foot above me, something that looked like me but it appeared drawn and pale. Smoke connected its head to mine. It became aware that she was looking at it, and it pulled away from me, thrusting its snarling face and evil-looking eyes towards her. At this point she had started screaming and I had woken up.

We swapped places around in the bed, moving the pillows and cushions, thinking that this would take our minds off what had happened. After a long time we managed to go back to sleep. When I awoke in the morning I sat up and pulled on the sleeve of my nightshirt. Over the main vein on my right arm there were two blood blisters that hadn't been there the day before.

The following night, I felt a presence in the bedroom again, not accompanied by a smell this time. Although I was properly awake, I felt a strong wave of lethargy pass through me. My mind was filled with thoughts of wanting to go to sleep, but I fought against them. *I didn't want to go to sleep*. The urge to lie down and return to my slumber got stronger and stronger... A wee voice in my head was telling me there was nothing there... that this wasn't real...

My girlfriend stirred, sat up and asked me what was wrong. I told her 'nothing' and suggested she go back to sleep, which she did. I felt that I needed to deal with this visitor alone, and without interference, or it would return again at another time.

Whatever it was after, it was trying to convince me that this was all in my imagination, and to just go back to sleep like my girlfriend. There were accompanying waves of tiredness and I used all my thoughts as resistance towards it. Then it made its fatal mistake.

As though it was my own thought inside my head I heard, "If this is real I should deal with it by projecting pictures of crosses, graveyards, concrete angels, and Christian symbols..." At which point I said aloud, "That stuff doesn't work for me, *but this does*!"

I pointed straight out in front of me with my right forefinger, and in the air I designed a reverse pentacle (a banishing spell that I had been taught). I found myself saying loudly,

"Get ye hence all things that are foul and profane, or you'll be forever cast into the outer reaches of darkness!"

At that point my girlfriend woke up from the noise of my raised voice and sat up. We both shivered as the room turned cold, and we witnessed a shimmer ahead of us as something seemed to disappear out of the room through the wall.

My girlfriend was concerned and wanted to know what it was. I explained that the 'thing' from the night before had come back. She was more than a little miffed that I hadn't alerted her, but she understood that I needed to face it alone and I didn't want her to become involved for fear it would hurt her.

What it was, I still don't know. It didn't come back the next night and I have never seen it again since. Now, more than three decades later, I have never forgotten this disturbing experience.

Preparation

Kate F

When I was eighteen I attended a local college to study drama, it was two towns over from my village. Unfortunately, my best friend Kirstie was attending university in a different location. We were able to synch our schedules and arrange nights out when she was back in the village with her parents, and when I didn't have any rehearsals on. This was one of those nights.

Kirstie's parents lived a five minute walk from my parent's house, in a 1980s development. My house was an Edwardian red brick semi-detached on the main street, opposite the Victorian village school. Although it was a main road, all of the houses were set back with their own front gardens, driveways and pretty sash windows. These houses didn't have numbers; they had quaint names such as 'The Laurels' and 'Snowdrop Villa'.

Overall my part of the village had a rich history. Even the inn opposite us had once been a blacksmith's forge in 1762. You could say that this little corner of the village was picture-postcard perfect. Any ghostly tales were reserved for the larger pub at the top of the village, where many spooky sightings had been recorded by the landlords and patrons over the decades.

It's important to note that, while I believe in the possibility of ghosts or spirits, Kirstie is very pragmatic and logical. She is interested in the theory of a spectre, but she certainly doesn't believe in them in the way that a ghost hunter or spiritual person does.

On this particular evening we had decided to give the slow-pace of village life a miss. Our game plan was to get dressed up and visit the local town, go to a pool hall and then on to a club for some dancing. Kirstie was driving us there so we were both planning on being sober, just enjoying the atmosphere.

Getting ready for me was a challenge. I had to fit my preparation around the rest of my family's busy schedule - this night out prep was just when everything would be happening in the household, late afternoon. I lived with my parents and my younger teenage sister.

At the time she was getting ready to go to her boyfriend's house, Mum was walking around trying to write a grocery shopping list so she could go to the supermarket (a twenty minute drive away) and my Dad had just got in from his long commute home after working in London all day.

I decided to wait until they'd gone their separate ways so that I could actually get the chance to have a shower in peace! An hour or so went by, so by now this would have been about quarter past six. It was during the summer and so it was still full daylight outside.

My sister was picked up by her boyfriend's parents; she wouldn't be back until Sunday. My parents called out 'goodbye' and got into the car to make the long trek to the supermarket through rush-hour traffic. At last I was alone and I could get things done.

I wasn't scared of being in the house by myself;

usually I would have found a CD to listen to. For some reason, this time, I was just so focussed on getting ready to meet Kirstie that I pulled my clothes from the wardrobe in my bedroom, dumped them on the bed, and turned the shower on to heat up, without putting any music on.

My mobile phone beeped and I realised I was low on battery. I walked downstairs and put the handset on to charge, plugged in next to the kitchen table. Our kitchen was downstairs at the back of the house in a new brick extension.

As soon as I was upstairs, I jumped into the steamy shower and thought about what songs I would request from the DJ at the nightclub, and whether or not I'd beat Kirstie at pool. Several minutes went by and I heard the front door click. I assumed it was my sister or parents coming back for something they had forgotten. But there were no footsteps inside the house.

I dismissed it as just a general 'house noise'. Then it clicked again. I could have sworn I heard the door open and then came the sound of faint footsteps. At this point I knew it wasn't my family members returning as they would have moved heavily on the old wooden floor boards...

My worst fear was that it was someone trying to break in, seeing that the car wasn't parked outside, thinking the house was empty. I was alone in the shower upstairs with no lock on the door, and no potential weapon. I desperately strained my ears above the noise of the running water to see if I could hear any other footsteps. Again there was nothing.

I waited for what seemed like forever. I heard nothing else, not even the front door closing. I assumed that it was my over-active imagination and it could have just been the creaks and groans of our old house as it cooled down from being in the hot sun all day.

I finished showering and wrapped a towel around me, I was half expecting to see the front door hanging open as I passed by the top of the stairs and looked down into the hallway... thankfully it was shut and all the lights I'd left on were still on. Nothing had changed at all.

As I walked back across the landing towards my bedroom, I nearly screamed. Out of the corner of my eye, in the hallway below I saw something move; something in the shape of a dark figure. We didn't have any pets and there was no sound of floorboards creaking this time. I suddenly felt very cold. As I dashed the few remaining feet to my bedroom door, I thought I saw the figure look up at me.

I slammed my bedroom door, heart pounding, and when I looked at my bedside table - where my phone would usually be - I nearly cried! It was downstairs in the kitchen... downstairs where I had seen that 'thing'. All my clothes were laid out on the bed, so I quickly dried myself and pulled on my jeans and glittery top. I shoved all of my make-up and hair products into a plastic bag and threw on a jumper. My hair was still soaking wet against my neck and shoulders.

All I kept thinking was: 'there is someone or something downstairs'. It played over and over again in my mind. I hadn't heard any noises on the stairs, but then again, when the figure moved it was nearly silent.

I checked my clock. About ten minutes had gone by. I wasn't supposed to meet Kirstie for ages. I knew she was getting ready at her house, catching up with her parents and brother. I didn't want to annoy her... I had to get downstairs to my phone.

After another five minutes spent listening for any creaks or clicks, I plucked up the courage to run down through the house to the kitchen. Opening my bedroom door took all the strength I had - I was sure that the 'thing' would be on the landing waiting to get me. All the lights were still on, there were no shadows... I guess that's what helped me push past my fear.

I nearly fell down the stairs, carrying my toiletries in one hand and my handbag in the other. I careered through the open-plan dining room in the exact spot where I had locked eyes with the figure. Still I didn't see anything untoward. I jumped into the kitchen and shut the dining room door behind me, bile rising in the back of my throat from the sudden exertion.

I checked the back door was locked and then I fumbled for my phone which, thankfully, was fully charged. Without thinking I rang Kirstie, usually we would always text message each other. The first call rang out and I tried again three times, each time feeling more and more anxious.

Finally she picked up and she could hear that something was wrong. I didn't want her to think I was making up a story, or being immature, so I just asked if I could finish getting ready at her house. She agreed, later telling me that she could tell how shaken I was.

Now, remember I told her nothing.

I just asked if I could go to her house and she said she would pick me up in her car to go the short distance.

Usually she would arrive outside and beep the horn or text me to say 'come out'. This time, because of how I sounded on the call, she came to the front door to meet me. The knocker went and I realised that I would have to make my way through the dining room and into the hallway to get to the front door.

Knowing that my best friend was at the other end of this gauntlet made it slightly easier. I made sure I had my phone and all my necessary belongings. I took my house key from the hook. I opened the dining room door and, thank God, there was nothing there; just a brightly lit room, wooden chairs, table and fireplace... all as they had been. No shadowy figure.

I darted through and opened the door for Kirstie. She stepped into the hall-way. When she asked me what was wrong I just brushed her off with a generic remark along the lines of: 'I just scared myself, that's all'. At that moment there was a creak on the landing above us. I jumped slightly. I was desperate to just get out of the door. She started to ask me some questions and kept looking behind me.

In the end I pretended to be calm and told her we just needed to get out of the house. I was sort of herding her out of the door. Kirstie walked out and I joined her, slamming the front door behind me - not caring if I'd even set the security lock.

We sat in her car in silence for a minute or so before driving back to her parent's house. I must admit, I didn't look back at my house, illuminated from the inside, for fear of what I would see silhouetted in one of the windows. All I know is, when I saw that *'thing'* it was very human-like and definitely real. It was almost as if it was a solid core of matter with dark inky smoke around it that formed the muscle.

Preparation

Kirstie B

(transcribed)

I lived down the road from you and we were going out. I mean actually *out* out, into town of an evening. I guess we might have been going to Jumping Jacks or Ikon [night clubs]. I think it was 'Cheesy Tuesdays' club night where they played all stuff like Blur, Nirvana, and then lots of songs that everyone knew like ABBA and some eighties bangers. I remember that we went there all the time, so this was quite normal. We weren't into the rave scene or anything like that.

I do remember that it was daylight though, so it must have been an evening in the summer. We might have been going out about seven-ish, so all this would have been around half five or six. I was just about to do my make up, I had done my hair, and I was thinking: 'Right, I'm almost done then I'll go down and pick Kate up'.

I was due to pick you up outside your house at, say, quarter past six. We were just going to jump in the car and go straight to town. It was literally the usual case of: I pull up, I'll wait outside your driveway in my car, and we go. We did it all the time that's how I knew how much time I had to get ready.

Then you rang me, let's say it was at quarter to six.

It was early, and you were like, "Yeah...uh... Kirst, are you alright?"

I was like, "Yeah, I've just got to do my make-up."

When you were talking to me, you sounded really 'fake happy', like you were faking being calm. Then you said: "Well, um, can you just come and get me now?" I was confused so I said: "I've got to do my make-up so, I'll literally be only ten or fifteen minutes, then I can come and get you and we'll go straight there."

Then you started sounding really weird and you said:

"Yeah, but, no, well, can you please come and get me now? I'll explain everything when you come, but can you come and get me right now please?" I've got to be honest Kate, you sounded really fucking weird at this point. You were acting really odd and I was a bit concerned. You asked me to come and get you so you could come back to mine and finish getting ready there.

I knew your mum and dad were out of the village doing the weekly shop at Tesco in town. So I drove down, pulled up outside your house and, for some reason, instead of waiting in my car I thought I'd get out and come and knock on your front door to let you know I was there.

You opened up the door, and when I looked up, on the top of the stairs, behind where you were standing in the downstairs hallway, I saw your sister Jo... or so I thought. 'She' was walking the last few steps up the stairs to the landing bit, across the landing and I heard the footsteps on the creaky floorboards. She was going towards your front bedroom. I was like,

"Oh, is Jo in tonight?" But you were ushering me out the door, saying

"No, no. I'm here on my own. Let's go!" And I kept saying:

"But I just saw somebody - what? I don't understand?" I was so confused because I'd just seen Jo. I knew your parents were out and I had just assumed that person - or figure - was Jo as it's the only other person it could have been.

We left your house really quickly and you didn't say anything in the car, so I knew something was up because usually we chat non-stop. When we got back to mine, it was only then that I confronted you. I didn't know how to really ask you actually, so I sort of said 'what was *that*?'

You told me you'd heard stuff when you were in your bedroom (at the front of the house). You'd heard footsteps and bonking around noises and then I remember you said you were scared because you remembered 'shit, my phone's down in the back kitchen'. You were really worried because you couldn't get to it without going through the bit of the house where you'd heard the noises.

I *know* I saw something when I picked you up, I *know* I heard those footsteps. Another thing I remember is that I thought it was pretty rude of your sister to be going into your room while you were going out and, when I mentioned that to you (while you were trying to get me out of the house), you kept saying in the weird cheery voice: 'no I'm on my own'.

I honestly think I believed it was her so much that I nearly said 'Hi Jo how's it going?' but I had stopped myself because you were so flustered. You were literally shoving me back out of the front door. I can picture it all now, even. I realised, as we were standing there in your hall, that it wasn't Jo. It was my brain making that assumption. Like if I describe what it looked like I would tell you it was a dark 'shape', a figure that made footsteps. It didn't look like your sister or any person that I knew of. I don't really think it even had a 'face'.

Preparation Post Script

Kate F

(transcribed)

So Kirst, what you don't know - I don't think me and Mum have ever told anyone outside the family - is that around that time in the summer something else happened.

A couple of weeks after me and you saw whatever that thing was, I woke up in the middle of the night hearing a blood-curdling scream coming from my parent's bedroom above me. My dad was away on an archaeology dig, and my sister was staying over at her boyfriend's house again.

I had college the next day and I had been up watching a film on Channel Four on the little TV in my bedroom, some comedy or something so I wasn't scared or thinking about what had happened with us. I didn't know what the time was but it was pitch black, and because we didn't have smart phones back then I couldn't see my phone screen or an alarm clock, I assumed it was early morning.

I have never been so terrified, I thought someone had broken into the house and my mum was getting murdered. It was like an animalistic, instinctual scream. It didn't even sound like screams you hear in horror films, it was disgusting. Then once that stopped (I was hiding under my duvet) I called up to her.

Then, in the same kind of 'fake cheery' voice which I spoke to you in, she said:

"It's okay, there's just a man at the top of my stairs. He was walking towards the bottom of my bed, but I'm alright." She later told me that she had woken up and been a bit sleepy, and seen a dark figure coming up her spiral stairs to the bedroom on the top floor.

She had assumed it was my dad coming home unexpectedly from the archaeology dig instead of staying at the campsite he'd organised. When she actually looked at the figure it wasn't my dad, and she thought someone was going to get her and that's why she started screaming. Then the figure disappeared.

We were both quite shaken after that and it was worse because my dad was staying away for two weeks, so really it was just me and my mum in the house on our own. She said that she knows it wasn't sleep paralysis, and she's had the feeling before of coming to from sleeping because then she's made a noise like snoring, or sleep talking. She says it wasn't anything like that at all. She genuinely felt someone had come in and we were being burgled or worse.

Preparation Final Comment

Lynne F

Over the years Kate has told me things that she has seen and heard at our house; some disturbing, some strange. Maybe a few can be de-bunked but the majority cannot and remain inexplicable. I believe her. I believe that she is especially sensitive to these things, whereas I have only had a few strange experiences; all of them relatively benign other than this particular one.

What happened that night has stayed with me. It was so terrifying that I try not to call it to mind; especially as I still live in the same house and sleep in that same bedroom. I remember Kate shouting, screaming up to me: 'Mum! Mum! Are you OK? What's happening?'. I remember thinking in that moment that I am her mum so I have to be the grown-up and tell her that I am fine. But, of course, I was not at all fine.

I had turned on my bedside lamp, my heart was pounding and I was having great difficulty trying to make sense of what I'd just been through. It was real yet I couldn't believe it had happened to me. I thought that nobody would take me seriously if I told them about it; although maybe they would as I'm not one given to having hysterics or telling melodramatic stories about myself.

This incident was very clear and simple and so is straightforward to recount.

My husband was away working at an archaeological site. At that time, it was usual for him to often be away for a week or two during the dig season. Kate and Jo had very full social lives and sometimes came back in the early hours or stayed over at their friend's houses. So I was used to being at home alone in the evenings and during the night. I never had concerns and I wasn't afraid of the dark.

That night was just like any other. I went to bed and fell asleep.

It was still night-time and so the room was in darkness, save for a little moonlight shining through the Velux window in the sloping ceiling. The stairs are about a metre from the end of my side of the bedframe.

I was awake and aware of a black figure at the top of the stairs. It was walking towards me. It was large, wearing a hat; definitely male. I could only see his shape, no detail of his face or clothing. I sensed he was powerful.

What happened next took seconds. So many thoughts came rushing through my mind at the same time. I said nothing; I couldn't, I was petrified and unable to move. My overriding thought and fear was that this man was an intruder and I was going to be attacked, and then Kate after me. The only escape routes were via the stairs, out of the Velux onto the roof, or out of the window to drop onto the ground from two floors up. I didn't know if I should attempt to save myself by taking one of these options. At the same time, I knew that I couldn't because I didn't want to leave Kate on her own in the house with him.

He was moving quickly towards me and I knew my time was up and I couldn't escape. I was overwhelmed by my terror and the evil, menacing atmosphere around him. I believed that he was going to attack me. I was aware that I was frozen to the spot, sitting in bed as he walked closer and closer to me.

He reached the foot of the bed and I thought to myself: 'This is it. He's going to kill me. I stared at him as he started to approach me then... he just disappeared.

At that moment I realised someone was screaming and that someone was me.

Next I heard Kate shouting up to me. I turned on my bedside lamp, still reeling from what I'd gone through. I tried to reassure Kate that everything was OK. I decided to leave the lamp on for the rest of the night and tried to go back to sleep.

I knew that I didn't want to start leaving the light on all night every time my husband was away. It was extremely difficult for me to turn it off during the next few nights, and for a long while after, that but I persisted.

Since then, the shadow figure has never returned to the bedroom and I've never experienced anything in the house like that again. On occasion when I think back to the incident, I am instantly taken back to that feeling of helplessness and absolute terror and, for a while, feel very wary when I go up to the bedroom on my own at night.

I am also reminded of what we were told when we bought the house. We were being shown around by the late owner's son, who had lived there for most of his life. He took us up to the attic room. He explained that the attic space hadn't been converted into a bedroom; it was a dedicated bedroom when the house was first built, hence the original window in the gable.

He said that the room had always been used for storage, other than when his uncle lived with them for a while and used it as his bedroom. I remember we left the viewing thinking it was odd that this man and his brother had shared the smallest bedroom in the house when this large attic room was available.

Sea Spirit

Maureen D

As a physical oceanographer I have spent my life studying the sea; watching every ebb and flow of the tide, scrutinising the horizon as it appears to fall off the edge of the world. One of my favourite parts of the job was to look at the properties of currents and swells. I had the opportunity to visit many different lands and be part of many different research projects.

That was in my past. My working life. I retired a few years ago. I'm now classing myself as full-time granny and master of laundry. I was hesitant about coming forward with my tale for fear I would be discredited among my peers. I have been promised anonymity, which encouraged me to be as open and honest as possible.

What I am about to describe really happened. I will use plain language so as not to confuse the situation. I also want to admit to wearing glasses, as I feel that this is a critical piece of information. When a person is describing a visual event, you need to be able to explore the possibility that their quality of eyesight played an integral part in how their brain perceived the situation.

At the time of writing this my age is sixty-eight, the event took place when I was in my late forties. I remember it was before my fiftieth birthday because I actually let slip half of the story to one of my family members when I was inebriated at my party! The next day I had to tell them it was just the drink talking... so Sal, if you read this - I'm sorry!

My tale begins in a place called North Wootten, near King's Lynn in Norfolk. It's considered a village, but it's not incredibly small. Most of the villages in that area had one or two streets lined with flint stone and red brick cottages. North Wootten was large enough to have several bed and breakfast establishments, its own medical centre and rugby club. When I arrived there, having left my home in Stoke-On-Trent, I was pleasantly surprised.

Being a woman of a certain age, I was all too aware of the 'funny' looks and whispered comments when I arrived alone in a new place. This was no exception. After a few days of milling around waiting for the rest of my team to turn up, I became accustomed to answering the "You here on your own then?" remarks. Luckily my colleagues were just as 'single' as me, varying in age from newly graduated students to sixty year old men.

The project we were embarking on was a study of an area called The Wash. There was to be an all-encompassing cataloguing of this part of the water and shore. It was being funded by a university in the UK, as well as several businesses based in Northern China. As a participant I was there to give my expert opinion on what was being documented, showing the graduates the ropes.

Physical oceanography can get, well, quite physical. It involves walking to the shoreline, taking boat trips out to sea, doing everything you need to do in all types of weather. North Norfolk in the depths of November can be very bleak! Huge steel-grey skies stretch out across milky brown swathes of salt marsh and sand. The wind is brutal if you don't have the right clothing!

I had come prepared, and by arriving early I had also gained a chance to find the best spots on the shore to start our introductory investigation. Some of the people on the team were not from the UK and, as with most working groups, the first days were a bit of a power struggle as we all sought to be heard and puffed our chests.

The weather wasn't as windy as I had anticipated (thank God) and I remember that a scarf wrapped around my neck and chin sufficed as protection from the elements, along with my trusty padded windbreaker. The main issue with the coastline in that part of the country is the treacherous incoming tide. The ground is so level, so unbelievably flat, that - as soon as the tide turns - water starts rushing back over the sand, heading for the plethora of narrow creeks that form a barrier between the land and the sea.

Many people have been caught unaware, it often makes national news when they become stranded, or sadly pass away. I had witnessed the danger myself many times at Holkham beach further along the peninsula. One minute you are standing there admiring the skyline, trying to spot cute furry seal pups... the next you are hopping around like a lunatic, trying to jump onto hummocks of sand as rivulets of saltwater gush in around your boots.

I found it amusing to see my colleagues being lectured on shore safety, when some of them probably had much more to worry about in their native lands. I wonder how much they paid attention to the team leader's tales of cockle-pickers swept away in an instant, when at home they were faced with poisonous creatures, sharks and cyclones!

We were a motley crew of folk, and I recall thinking that it would be a great challenge to bring us all to the same level of working practise. My fears were correct. After the first week of planning and gathering initial data we were already two days behind schedule. I had taken a shine to an older gentleman named Clive. He was from Ontario, Canada. He had a dry wit and was a dab-hand in his field, marine biology.

As two of the more senior members of the team we found ourselves drawn to each other, discussing previous excursions and comparing life experiences. On the first weekend, Clive suggested that we do a little exploring of the local area and see if there were any suitable research sites on the other, northern, side of The Wash, towards Skegness. I thought this was a splendid idea, and so we packed a picnic and headed off in my reliable old Vauxhall Corsa.

I don't know how long I was driving before I started to feel that I had a headache coming on. It was unusual as I have always enjoyed perfect health. Considering that I wanted to get to know Clive more, I suddenly found his comments irritating and I felt an immediate need to pull the car over and get out. It was the strangest sensation.

We were past the Frampton Marsh area. I think we were somewhere on our way to Butterwick. We weren't on the main road, for some reason I had taken a couple of single track roads and I could see the open water of The Wash to my right, beyond the salt marshes. I opened my window and the sea air immediately hit me, filling the car with a fresh scent. I hoped that would blow away my headache.

It didn't.

A few minutes later I hurriedly suggested we pull over and take a look down one of the tracks that led across the marshy area to the exposed sand. It was low tide and nearly lunch time so Clive didn't object.

The pounding in my head was so unusual that it left me almost mute. I felt that opening my mouth, using my facial muscles, was a great effort - heaven knows what I looked like to poor Clive! He had a rucksack with the food and drink in, whilst I carried an Ordnance Survey map. I was supposed to be marking where we had stopped, but I was just walking down to the beach as if in a trance. I don't have a clue what Clive spoke to me about. I just know that I had to get to the shore and...

This is where my intention becomes a little hazy. When I tell you the 'story' I want to justify it and say that I simply wanted to get a good view of the Norfolk side of The Wash, looking across the expanse of the wide bay back towards North Wootten. In reality - if I am being truthful and transparent - my intention was to walk to the beach and keep going; walking into the sea as if I was impervious to water. I had to keep walking to a point somewhere out in the waves. If I reached that location I knew my headache would dissipate and I would feel at ease.

As I had previously mentioned, this was November. Britain is not famed for its warm winters. I can't fathom (if you'll excuse the pun) why on earth I had any inclination to step into those freezing waters, let alone encourage them to wash over me. Drown me. I understand, as a rational hindsight driven narrator, that I would have been killed had I walked into the North Sea; home to desolate oil rigs, Doggerland and darkness.

Anyway, I digress. At the time I was heading for the yellow mustard sand, still slick from the receding tide and spray. We had walked through the cluster of low marsh foliage and muddy inlets. We were now on the beach proper. Clive was stooping down every so often to look at the small pieces of debris washed up; a few razor shells, some weed, and other minute flotsam. As he kept hesitating I was striding on ahead.

I had assumed the tide was fully out at this point, but I believe it may have only been half way as there was not as much sand as the usual mile or more trek to the water's edge. The wind was low, the waves lapped gently, and the water was more blueish green than muddy brown. The cloudy sky seemed to give the scene a bright enhancement - like a studio photographer's lighting.

The 'headache' I was experiencing had not subsided, but it had changed. Evolved. Morphed. It occupied a constant throbbing, almost melodic space inside me. I felt it in my temples, like a net over the back of my skull. Amidst the pulsing and tingling sensation was something I could barely make out. It was a voice.

I was at the water's edge. I was wearing traditional leather walking boots and jeans tucked into thick woollen walking socks. I didn't have wellingtons on, and I certainly wasn't wearing waders. The next thing I remember is Clive appearing beside me and gently pulling me back saying something along the lines of, "Surely you don't want wet feet this early on!"

I heard him as if through a fog, a mist. It was distant and sluggish. I knew exactly where I was on the beach. I was perplexed as to why he had pulled me away from my goal. I don't think I replied to him. I stepped back towards the tide and water slapped the toes of my boots again. It soaked in under the laces and I remember thinking (as if I was two people), 'That's freezing cold!' Then at the same time, 'This is the beginning, it will get better'...

The voice was becoming clearer; it was more of a sensation - like a telepathic voice. It was saying 'come unto me' over and over. It was very hypnotic and rhythmic; like something you would hear in a modern health resort spa, accompanied by whale song and tribal instruments. Here it was joined by the swish of the waves hitting the sand, the rush of cool air. It was a sad, haunting voice...

The issue I take with this paranormal experience is the 'voice'. If I was suddenly, irrevocably compelled to walk towards a beautiful stretch of water I could reconcile that as a mental health 'need', or a strange moment that I was going through brought on by stress and a new environment. But hearing voices, feeling hypnotised - this was more than just low blood sugar levels, or a momentary lapse of reason.

Clive tried to pull me away again, showing me a couple of shells he had picked up that interested him. The only thing that interested *me* was the origin of the voice. I stood stock still, and I tried to explain, reply to his conversation, yet when I opened my mouth my speech was slurred and in my own head my vocal chords resonated as if they were in harmony. At this point I believe he realised there was an issue and helped me to sit down on the damp sand.

I continued to stare out to sea and in the middle distance I saw the familiar head of a grey seal bobbing above the surf. Its small black eyes were connecting with mine. This was not an unusual occurrence, and Clive pointed it out. I guess he was trying to lighten the mood. I was transfixed. As I watched the seal's mottled head swaying in the water I saw something else.

It was covered in flecks of green, the colour of the darkest seaweed I had come across. It had long flowing black 'hair' and it appeared to be swimming around the seal. It had a human-like appearance, but due to the green speckled flesh it was hard to make out its form. Clive shielded his eyes and stood up.

"Hey, there's someone out there!" he suddenly shouted.

He looked around the beach for a sign of abandoned clothing or belongings. The safety briefing must have been fresh in his mind.

I knew instinctively that this was not a person. My headache was becoming more acute and the voice was almost painful to hear. It was now reduced to a single word "Come, come, come!" My dual mentality allowed me to remain seated and yet still feel the urge to fling myself into the waves and meet this creature.

Clive shouted a few more times, cupping his hands

around his mouth and waving both his arms. The seal disappeared beneath the surface and I caught a glimpse, more directly, of the green beast's face. Its eyes were in the same place as a human - yet they were black like a seal's. The nose appeared as two slits, flat against the face, again, like a seal. The hair was thick and waist-length. The torso was that of a man, but freckled with dark green markings around the shoulders, with a paler green underbelly.

Just at the very moment I feared I could stand the voice no longer, Clive shouted at the creature that he'd call the coastguard for assistance. It was a booming yell, his voice breaking slightly. The creature could easily hear it as there was no wind to carry the sound away. Immediately the voice in my head turned into a shrill shriek! It was like a condensed, compact scream of frustration and anger. No more than a few seconds. Maybe even a split second.

Silence.

Clive was panting slightly and looking out to sea, his hands clamped to his brow creating a shade for his eyes, peering at where the seal and the figure had been. I stood up and he turned to me, concern written over his face.

"You saw that? Shouldn't we do something? Have you got the coastguard's number?"

I assured him that it was just a couple of seals next to a buoy. The weed and angle of the waves must have made it appear like a person was in distress. He asked me how I could be so sure... and I said the only thing I could.

"I'll never be a hundred percent sure, but I'd also never risk a person's life." This seemed to satisfy him.

He sat back down next to me and told me about his excursions in Newfoundland, and how seals were easy to spot in the icy waves. My head was clear, my senses had returned to normal, there was no residual drowsiness. I suggested we open our box of sandwiches as I felt a little hungry. He mentioned my odd behaviour and I fobbed him off with an excuse about a sugar crash from the chocolate cake I had eaten for breakfast instead of cereal. He didn't pursue the matter further and our day continued as planned.

*   *   *

That night, driving back to the village I felt extremely tired. It was the sort of exhaustion one experiences when adrenaline has left the body after there has been a high alert situation such as a trauma or accident.

I have tried to play out the experience in my head time and again. I put different emphasis on different parts, attempting to come up with a plausible explanation. The most believable reasoning would be what I told Clive; it was a buoy, a couple of seals and some tangled seaweed. There was no green speckled figure with black hair and jet-coloured soulless eyes. I was having a sugar-crash, I was dehydrated and my compulsion to walk into the sea upon hearing a 'voice' was simply tinnitus and hazy thinking...

I have never been able to fully get on board with this theory. Researching tales from mariners - stretching back as far as written records go, and beyond - they speak of sirens; spirits of the sea that call to sailors and land dwellers alike. Some suggest they are beautiful women, some suggest they have malignant intent. All I can be sure of is the thing I saw, and the ethereal voice I heard.

Whether or not you believe me is not something I can control.

Black Object In The Sky

Gavin H

I've been interested in astronomy since childhood, inspired by science fiction. I've been intrigued by the idea that on some distant star there is another astronomer looking back at me. I have always been open to the possibility of alien life around another star, but thought the distances involved were too large for any being to visit Earth. While I was fascinated by reports of UFOs (and open-minded about the more compelling cases), I had a filter of scepticism - especially for hoax videos.

During my time watching the sky I had seen many mysterious lights, shapes and reflections. I was able to identify them as aircraft, animals or explainable aerial phenomena. For me the reality of *unidentified* aerial phenomena was about to change...

It was a Sunday evening, the 31st of May, at about eight o'clock. It was still light. The sky was clear. I was travelling back to Leicester. My father was driving and my mother was in the back. The car had a large sunroof and it was possible to look straight up through it. We were travelling south on the M1. Having passed Junction 25, we were heading towards East Midlands Airport.

As I wasn't driving it gave me the opportunity to look for aircraft - on landing at East Midlands they pass directly over the motorway on their final approach. The airport was about three miles away and I noticed that an aircraft had just flown over the carriageway. I was a little disappointed as it meant there wouldn't be another one to spot for some time. Luckily, as the aircraft descended out of view and onto the runway, I could make out a black dot in the distance. It began to grow in size.

"There's a helicopter coming this way. Look." my father remarked. As he had to keep his eye on the road he wasn't able to observe it fully as it came closer. I was expecting the black shape to resolve into a helicopter. I'd seen distant aircraft look mysterious before; they usually became more recognisable as they approached.

This aircraft did not.

It retained its black appearance and unusual shape. I felt circuits within my brain quickly attempting to recognise and conceptualise what this object was as it came closer. It was flying approximately three hundred feet above the northbound carriageway of the M1. If you were a driver on that road maybe you wouldn't give a second thought to a dark shape passing through your peripheral vision. You would be concentrating on maintaining your speed and position in your lane. I, on the other hand, had the opportunity to stare at this object without interruption.

It was approximately seven feet tall and seemed to have a single fin protruding from its starboard side. It was very black and I found it difficult to make out its shape. It did not appear to have any depth, mass or reflective material. It was as if a piece of the sky had been cut out. I leant forward in my seat. It was almost above us by this point. There seemed to be no features, markings or texture to its surface. There were no windows, vents, exhausts or plumes of hot gas.

The colour was uniform over its surface like it was absorbing light. I had the impression that there weren't any occupants; the object appeared too small. It had an eerie 'indifferent' quality about it, but at the same time I had the feeling that I didn't want to attract its attention. While staring at it I struggled to distinguish and comprehend what I was seeing. "Is this for real? What am I looking at? Is this it? Is it finally my time to see a real UFO? Surely not!".

I considered all the options. Was it an aircraft? Was it a bird? A black bag caught on the wind? A piece of debris carried in a slipstream? The obvious explanation is that it was some kind of advanced 'black project', maybe a customised drone. However, you would expect even an advanced object to look like a piece of technology that I could somewhat recognise...

By now it was overtaking traffic on the opposite carriageway. I had seen it approach from several miles away and it was still holding its speed, at an altitude of what seemed to be three hundred feet. It flew above the car. I had a good view of it from underneath - but again I could not see any features except that disconcerting otherworldly black skin.

I watched it turn away from the M1 and begin to make its way over the fields toward Manchester. I tried to forget about it as I really needed to continue my journey to Leicester, there was no time to take a different route and investigate further. Later, as I reflected on the experience, I realised that I had seen something remarkable. It seemed like a missed opportunity as I had wanted to brush it off as a misidentified mundane object.

My great regret was that in my pocket I had a mobile phone with a camera and I never thought to use it! I also found it a little disturbing that the object appeared near an aircraft landing at East Midlands Airport. I often wonder if it was noticed there. I have seen videos of similar objects on YouTube that notably interact with a civilian aircraft and it's on board systems.

When I discuss my experience with other people some are genuinely interested and do not deny the strangeness of this object. Some have suggested the more disturbing idea that it could have been a demonic presence. I'm often surprised by the hostility of some people's reactions, as if it contradicts the reassuring premise that humans are in charge and leaders of the universe.

I do not claim to know what this object was, just that it was real. Incidents like this are not as remarkable as people imagine; which is possibly why they are missed or ignored in everyday life.

The White Lady

Kirstie B

(transcribed)

I was recently doing some digging into sleep paralysis, after randomly watching a documentary about it on TV. After I had read a few articles I suddenly remembered something from my childhood that I had rationalised out as something sleep or dream related, but now I'm not so sure.

It was when I was driving up to see my extended family in Scotland, with my parents and brother. We always used to stop off in the Lake District and stay overnight, just to break the journey up a bit for my dad, who was the main driver. This time around we were lodging at this inn; it was called 'The Black Sheep' or something like that. It was cheaper than a bed and breakfast. I can't really remember much, other than it was around the Kendal area.

So we arrived, unpacked, had a meal in the bar bit, then we all went off to bed. Me and my brother had a room together, we had twin beds because at that point we were too old to share a bed. Mum and Dad had a double room across the little corridor from us. Each of the rooms had its own en suite bathroom and toilet, and those rooms backed onto each other, sharing a wall.

All of this happened around April time, because we were going up at Easter specifically, for a special meal and family get-together. This was round about the year

2003. I was a young adult, and my brother was in his late teens. The inn looked as if it could have been built in the 1600s, it was really, really old with dark beams and white plaster ceilings.

Me and my brother had got off to sleep fine, there were no issues and the beds were comfortable. As it was late spring the sun started coming up at a reasonable time in the morning, I believe it was about five o'clock. It was gloomy in the room, and outside it was that strange half-light you get in the morning before the sun's up properly.

It made the room seem even darker.

I turned over in my bed, and I just remember laying there and feeling this utter 'terror'.

I was really, really scared, but I didn't know why. It was a feeling that washed over me for no reason. Absolute terror and fear – it's the only way I can describe it.

Then as I rolled over again, thinking 'what on earth's going on?' I glanced down so I wasn't looking at the ceiling anymore. At the foot of my bed by the window was the figure of a lady. She was wearing a white lace dress of some description, but the strangest thing was that I couldn't make out her facial features.

It was like she was a mannequin, one of those stylised ones where they don't have a face. It was just nothing, white. There was no other detail around her face or anything, other than the embroidery of her dress; I could actually see the patterns in the lace. I would say it looked like a wedding gown, but it might not have been for that purpose. It could have just been a pretty dress.

She was stood there, didn't move, didn't do anything, didn't say anything. She was like a statue just standing there in the gloomy bedroom. I didn't say anything either because I kept thinking to myself 'this isn't right, it can't be happening, I must be making it up'.

It was as if the terror that I felt had come first, before I even clocked that there was anything there in the room, if that makes sense. It was like I came out of my sleep because of the feeling of terror and I was frightened, *then* I saw her there. Not the other way around.

Well, I thought 'this isn't right, I'm not having this, I'm obviously seeing things'. I reached across to turn on the bedside light that was on the little nightstand between the two beds. I turned the lamp on, and as I looked across at my brother expecting him to wake up and complain that a bright light was near his face... he was already awake.

He was staring across at the corner of the room next to the window, past the foot of my bed. The same corner I had been looking at. By this point the lamp lit up the room, and I could see there was nothing there. He looked at me, and I asked:

"Did you -"

But neither of us felt like we wanted to speak, or verbalise what had happened. It still felt as if 'it' was in the room, still there with us. So I tried to ask again, through my facial movements, raising my eyebrows, indicating with the direction of my eyes to the corner. He just said:

"Yeah... but I don't know what that was..."

He was really dismissive, although his face looked like he was scared or shocked, with big open eyes and dilated pupils despite the bright lamp. I asked him if we could leave the light on for a couple of hours rather than having the room dark until it was time to get up for breakfast. He agreed without hesitation, and said we should leave it on. Usually he preferred a dark room to sleep in, so that was odd.

It was like neither of us could speak freely, we had to try and act 'normally' in case the woman, the 'thing', picked up on it and realised we were talking about her. I can't explain it, I was just aware that I needed to not acknowledge what had happened. By looking at my brother's expression we both felt that way, even though we hadn't discussed it.

We lay there for another hour or so, neither of us sleeping. Eventually we got up and started getting dressed and showered. We went down to breakfast and the landlord who served up the meal was making small talk with us, asking how our night had been.

Of course we'd already told our parents what we had seen, and they were *extremely* dismissive. They didn't believe us in the slightest, even though we both told them the same thing. My mum, a logical, straight-talking Glaswegian, said that I had just been imagining it. So when she had a chance to tell this 'funny story', she explained to the landlord what we had seen in the bedroom.

She expected him to roll his eyes, chuckle, and agree with her that it was all an overactive imagination, straight away he stopped and said:

"Oh? Was that the white lady then?"

I did a double take and my mum was also surprised. He told us that she'd been known to walk between the two bathrooms, and walk in and out of the bedroom we were staying in.

He went on to tell us that when the inn was built it was used as a judicial building, a bit like a court house. They would hold rudimentary trials there, and they used to convict the people in the building, then take them outside to be hung in a big oak tree (which was positioned at the end of the modern-day car park).

He explained that a lot of the people hadn't actually done anything wrong, or if they had it was a petty crime. He always assumed that she was probably the spirit of somebody who was wrongly judged, and then was being held for execution - which sometimes could take up to three days to go through, which was why she wandered the rooms.

Looking back on what he said, and how I had felt when I woke up, I wonder if that feeling of terror was actually me picking up on the feeling of dread emanating from her as she waited to be executed.

The reason why I don't think it was sleep paralysis or just sleeping in an unusual setting that caused me to see something odd, is because I was able to move. I didn't feel trapped or immobile. Also, my brother exhibited the same reactions and facial expressions as me. And neither of us knew the history of the inn before the next morning. We just assumed it was like any other hotel or pub that had boarders.

If you think I could have read something online, or overheard someone in the bar when we were eating in the evening, then that's always a very slim possibility. From what I remember, I just thought we were staying at a cheap place, no back story, and we were having a fun road trip as a family.

I'd like to go back there and see if anything happens again, but maybe not on my own!

Reeling

Sandra W

This is a simple straightforward description of a moment that was neither simple nor straightforward.

We live in a little Edwardian semi-detatched house which has been here since 1903. The land that the houses along our road occupy was formerly a field. The layout of the original part of the house has only been changed in one respect since it was built. There used to be a tiny passageway that divided the current dining room. On one side of this partition wall was the original kitchen, on the other side was the open staircase.

The previous owner explained to us that the passage was too narrow for his mother to wheel a traditional pram through so, sometime in the 1930s when this young couple were updating the property, the wall was taken down. His father also removed the bannisters and handrail from the stairs, then put up a wooden tongue and groove wall which concealed them and created a cupboard underneath. In our turn, decades later, we adapted this idea by putting in new tongue and groove panelling over the understair cupboard area and reinstated the bannisters and handrail.

The whole space is much brighter; sunlight penetrates all the way to the stairs from the dining room window. On entering the house you can now walk unobstructed from the front door, along the short hallway, past the bottom of the stairs and through the dining room to the new kitchen extension.

Why have I concentrated on describing this mundane scene? I've given this level of detail because I want you to picture the floor plan. 'It' happened in that particular place; the part of the house that had been the narrow passageway and is now the main route through our dining room.

One day, I was in the kitchen doing the usual chores and my husband was upstairs. As I walked through the dining room, I noticed a reel of sticky tape on the floor in front of me. I automatically picked it up, put it back on the table and continued to the front room.

A few steps later, my mind caught up with what I had seen. The reel had not just been 'on the floor'. It had been standing *upright* on the floor, balanced on the width of the tape. I asked myself how it could have fallen off the table and landed in that position... Then, immediately after that I questioned how it could have fallen off the table in the first place, seeing as I always lay reels down flat on their side. Peculiar.

Of course, my husband must have thought it funny to place the reel there. I called up to him. He wandered part-way down the stairs and looked at me from over the handrail. I asked if he'd been messing about and playing some sort of game with me. He had no idea what I was talking about. He insisted he'd been upstairs for ages in the study. I could tell that he wasn't winding me up.

Everything began to sink in and we looked at each other, puzzled. No radio had been playing, the house was quiet. It dawned on me that I hadn't heard the sound of anything falling onto the floor. Neither of us knew how to explain the strange position of the tape. I said that maybe I should have taken a photo of it, as evidence, before I picked it up...

I corrected myself straight away. That would have been daft; that wouldn't have proved anything. It would merely have been a photo of a reel of tape balancing on the floorboards. And that's another thing; our house is old and the floor is uneven. It's incredibly unlikely that if the tape for some reason had been standing on end, then rolled onto the floor and landed silently, that it would have remained upright.

At the time, and whenever I bring the moment to mind since, I feel as if the tape was deliberately put there for me to find. It was on the section of floor that had once been the narrow passageway. It had been positioned perfectly in the centre of my path, on the wooden floorboards between the edge of the rug and a wooden chest; precisely placed and beautifully balanced, waiting for me.

All I know for sure is that it happened.

Make of it what you will.

You Suck!

Jo R

I was about fifteen years old, so this was 2001ish. My sister was older than me and at college, but on the days she didn't have lectures we would watch TV together after I came home from school. We always sat on the settee in our small front room and waited for Neighbours to come on. It was a crap soap opera but, hey, I was a teenager.

We used to get really frustrated because some days the educational kids programme Blue Peter would be shown beforehand and, being older than the target audience, it seemed really boring to us. One of these times we were sitting there, munching on some crisps, when I decided it would be funny to shout at the TV.

I don't know why I did it; I just thought I would make my sister laugh. We still had a CRT old style TV. It could probably have taken me throwing a cushion at it - but I didn't want to risk it. So I just said really loudly something like 'You suck!' and, of course, my sister laughed. I laughed... but neither of us expected what happened   next.

The presenter 'came out' of the scene she was doing on Blue Peter, looked directly into one of the cameras, and said,

"No I don't."

I jumped up out of my seat and checked with my sister, who was also staring open-mouthed at the screen. I started to ask her -

"You saw that right? *You saw her say that!*" I felt sick. This was too strange, so we switched onto a different channel and sat there in silence.

We only had terrestrial TV channels so there was no way to rewind it or find a copy of it, but I have never understood what happened. I'll paint the Blue Peter scene for you, before she broke the fourth wall.

It was an overhead shot of the studio. There were some guests in, possibly kids doing some dancing or gymnastics. She was presenting with a co-host and the camera was panning around high above them as they stood at the edge of the performance area.

I am sure there was marching band music playing and that's also why this was shocking. When she looked straight into the aerial camera, it zoomed in on her slightly. It wasn't like she was already talking, or starting to do an intro to the next segment of the show.

She took two steps forward, looked directly into the camera, said 'No I don't', then stepped back. It was all over in a couple of seconds but I'll never forget it.

Evening Walk

Karen S

In 1997 I was living in a village in Dorset with my now ex-husband and three teenage children. The youngest had just started secondary school in Lyme Regis, while the other two were quite a way over where we used to live in Bridport. I spent my free time being a taxi driver between schools, running the family, and generally being invisible.

As I could tell my marriage was going down the pan (my husband was spending more and more time in London on 'business'), I decided to get the family a dog. I naively assumed that we could all go on weekend walks together and it would bring back the closeness we had lost.

Of course, this didn't happen. I was always the one left planning walking routes, and trying to motivate everyone to get out of the house. One summer evening I had come to the end of my tether. The kids were arguing over a video game, my husband was shouting at them to 'grow up', and the dog was whining. In exasperation I suggested going for an evening hike to the hills. Surprisingly, no one objected!

I grabbed the dog's lead and car keys, we piled into the car, and I started to drive. I didn't really know where we should walk. It was already after seven, but being summer the sky was still light. I decided to drive up to a hill top site called Lambert's Castle. I sometimes went there for a circular, easy walk while the children were at school.

We reached the little car park area under some trees just quickly enough to prevent another outbreak of arguing from the children in the back. All three jumped out and started to complain that it was too cold, and that there was nothing to do. My husband decided to blame me for the excursion and walked off in the direction of the main grassy area at the centre of the castle.

This had once been an Iron Age fort; the wooden buildings had long since rotted away. All that was left were some well-trodden paths through short scrubby grass, and some woodland. Occasionally you are able to go downhill a bit and walk around the ramparts. These were just built-up layers of soil that had been used for defence, no stonework. It's all very natural.

I found myself standing by the car with the dog still in the boot, and my youngest hanging around unsure who to side with. Eventually he chose to walk with me and the dog. We followed my husband and the other two around the winding paths, they were chatting away. It slowly got darker as dusk fell. Instead of going back towards the car park, we had chosen a trail that led onto the tarmac road on top of the ridge.

The road had a wooden footpath sign that said another 'castle' was just a short walk away. My husband decided to stride on ahead and, as I was in no hurry to return to our fractious household, I followed suit. I didn't fully realise how dark it had become until I looked back towards Charmouth on the coast and saw that people had started turning their house lights on.

Some of the ships on the ocean also had lights on,

looking like tiny orange flecks of glitter on the dark blanket of the ocean. There were sheep and cows in the fields either side of the road so I kept the dog on a tight leash. It wouldn't stop whining and trying to buck forward. My husband was getting irritated so he came back and yanked the lead out of my hand, jogging onwards towards Coney's Castle.

The dog seemed happy enough to be going faster and my youngest son had walked over to one of the field gates where a sheep was eagerly licking his hand. It was a nice sight to see him so happy, a silhouette against the deep blue evening sky. I joined him at the gate, and we both leaned on it ruffling the sheep's heads as they came up to be petted, thinking we had food.

The field was on the inland side of the road, so we were looking out over rolling fields towards Pilsden Pen (the highest point in Dorset) on the opposite ridge. In the deep twilight we couldn't really make out any villages. Squinting down into this valley there was the occasional farmstead, but it was mainly fields. We decided to stay a bit longer and pet the five or so sheep that were now trying to nibble our fingers as we tore out clumps of grass for them from the verge.

After bending down and tugging on a particularly large tuft of grass, I nearly lost my balance. I used the field gate to haul myself up and the old metal squeaked a bit, which made the sheep scatter. My son was still leaning on the gate and he was staring intently ahead of him. I slowly became aware that something wasn't right.

Ahead of us, floating above the descending

hillside, maybe about fifty feet off the ground, was a black aircraft with multiple coloured lights on it. My first instinct was that it was a helicopter. It definitely wasn't a drone. In 1997 very few people had drones, and besides, it was *massive*.

Just as I had seen my son as a silhouette on the gate against the navy blue sky, this aircraft was a black, huge, rounded shape; like a large military helicopter. It had blue, red and green lights on it, and it was definitely hovering in one spot. The lights were muted. They weren't blinding us so I assume it wasn't facing us head on. I couldn't believe how close it was!

My son was transfixed and I must admit I was intrigued as it was so imposing. We didn't speak a word. We just leaned on the gate and watched it. After about a minute had passed the lights went out and the aircraft shot upwards, disappearing into the sky above us. We waited a few seconds but it didn't return.

I didn't really know what to say so I just suggested that we catch the others up, and I tried to ignore what we'd seen. After we had walked several yards, my son asked "If that was a helicopter... why couldn't we hear the blades and the motor?" It was then that it struck me. The aircraft had been completely silent, that's what was odd. It was so close to us but not a breath of wind or a sound had come from it.

My son went on to ask why there hadn't been a cockpit, and how it had gone upwards so quickly without causing a breeze. I was also questioning all of these points and I just couldn't comprehend what had happened.

We started to walk more quickly and caught up with the rest of the family. My son asked if anyone had seen the 'weird helicopter' and they all said 'no'. They had been under the trees at the edge of the other castle area, having their own conversation and playing with the dog.

I have occasionally thought about what I saw on that night. The lights didn't look like those of any aircraft I've seen since, or even any aircraft from a TV show or film. It had no reflective glass 'cockpit' area or a window. There was no sound at all. I just can't explain what it was.

Lights

Alex B

I want to tell you that my girlfriend made me submit this story. I don't actually know what I saw, but I can't explain it and neither can anyone else I told. So, I guess I'll put it out there and you can decide. She wants me to tell you the first bit (which I didn't know until later) because she says it will give some other view on what happened.

About a week before the main thing happened, which was when it was dark, something weird happened in the daytime on the same bit of land. This field is next to the M80 motorway between Glasgow and Cumbernauld. It's just at the part where Stepps village is. So if you look at a map it goes Stepps Village, some fields, then the motorway.

It was an overcast day and my girlfriend was in the passenger seat of the car while I was driving. We were headed towards Glasgow, because we were going over Loch Lomond way to take some photos of a waterfall. She had her camera out on her lap and was fiddling around with the settings.

Suddenly she lifted the camera up and started pointing it at something out of her window, but only for a few seconds. Then she got pissed off that it was 'too blurry' and put her camera away. She told me that what she had tried to film were a few strong lights coming through the clouds over the field, like search lights from a helicopter. She said they were a warm yellow colour and all moved independently. They were so strong that she could see them even though it was midday.

Apparently, because I was driving at sixty-five miles per hour and because there was dirt on the car window, the camera hadn't focussed when she zoomed in to film it. So nothing showed up apart from a bunch of blurry pale grey clouds for ten seconds. She didn't tell me any of this at the time.

Then a week later we are returning from Glasgow way, headed towards Cumbernauld. It was early evening and because it was winter the sky was already pitch-black. There are main lights on that bit of the motorway, then either side the fields are completely dark. There's one farm on that side which had some flood lights, but this was after the farm, where there are just fields.

I'm concentrating on the road ahead, there aren't many cars. Then I see out of my window in the distance a set of about three bright lights; like stadium floodlights, lighting up the field which is full of long grass.

My first thought is, must be a helicopter looking for someone on the run. Then when I drive closer I realise that the lights aren't moving. They are completely still, like they are on a frame of some kind... but that wouldn't work because they were about fifty metres up, maybe more. I can't see any frame or poles and the lights are so bright the whole field is lit up - can see all the bushes and stuff around the edges of it.

We don't have the radio on and we can't hear any noise like a helicopter or a plane. Then we drive past and I get a clear view, and there's definitely nothing there just these three massive floating, static lights. My girlfriend says "Can you see those?" and I say "Yep" because I am still trying to guess what they are and it wasn't normal.

We drive further on and she looks back, tells me they are still there. I felt a bit confused, like I could tell there was something different about them, but I can't explain it to you. When we got home she told me about the similar lights in the same place the week before, and that they were moving.

I assumed it was something to do with police, or the military or even an event like a concert. We checked social media and the news for days afterwards and there's no record of anything happening.

Bathtime

Linda N

In the early 1980s I was living in south London with my boyfriend. We shared a house with his sister and her partner. Although the property was divided into separate flats they did not have their own front doors. We just had a back door and a front door that opened onto the street. My boyfriend's parents lived in the house next door. The back garden fence had long been removed so that both households could share the outside space.

It was a mid-terrace Victorian property, originally built for army officers and their families; the Royal Artillery Barracks was within walking distance. It was just as you would imagine; a cellar, ground floor, first floor and two attic rooms. Our bedroom was in the attic alongside a kitchen area. We all shared the bathroom on the first floor.

Around that time playing squash became fashionable. It was a sport that anyone who was 'something in The City' would play after work, vying for some perceived dominance or other. Eventually, the craze filtered down to street level and squash courts were the place to go, if that was your thing. It was definitely not my thing.

On this particular evening everyone had arranged to go out to play squash, including my boyfriend's parents. Off they all went, leaving me on my own in the house, with next door empty too. I decided to make good use of that time by having a long bath. As usual, I needed to wind down after a very busy and stressful day at work. I recall that it must have been autumn or winter because it was already dark when they left.

I had been in the bath for a while; just lying there, letting my mind wander, occasionally topping up with hot water. The house was silent. I remember noticing that I was so very still that there was no sound of water lapping around me.

Then I became aware of footsteps.

Someone was walking around on the ground floor, along the hallway and in and out of rooms. My fight or flight mode immediately kicked in, while at the same time the sensible and practical side of my brain was trying to process what was going on. I knew that I had to remain calm in the water for as long as possible to give myself the best chance of working out what to do next.

Initially, I thought that maybe my boyfriend's parents were home and had let themselves in through the back door. But I hadn't heard the door open and, in any case, I'm sure they would have called up to me because they knew I would be there. They certainly wouldn't have been going into rooms without permission.

I told myself that maybe the sound had travelled from the other neighbouring property in the terrace, since our staircase and theirs was separated by nothing more than the width of an internal wall. That was not the answer either. The sound of the footsteps was not muffled. I was convinced it was the distinct, purposeful tread of a man on the hard flooring.

I was facing the open bathroom door, which led immediately to the top of the stairs. The landing light was not on. All I could see was that ominous pitch-black rectangle. I battled to keep my breathing as shallow as possible and concentrated on not making even the slightest movement. By now my ears were ringing. I could hear the rhythmic pulse of blood pumping around my body. I was desperate not to attract attention to myself.

I have a very vivid, terrifying memory of thinking that it would only be a matter of time before the intruder decided to explore the rest of the house. I had to decide if I wanted to be assaulted while naked in the bath, or at the top of the house where there would be no escape.

I am quite single-minded when the going gets tough, so being brave was my only option - the only way to give myself a slim chance of being able to fight back. There was nothing to hand that I could use as a weapon. I was certain that once I made a noise he would know that he wasn't alone in the house and then the attack would begin. I had to go for it.

I climbed out of the bath, wrapped a towel around myself and went through the doorway, along the landing and up the stairs to the bedroom. Somehow, I managed to walk; running would have immediately alerted him. My feet moved swiftly and soundlessly up the carpeted stairs. Sopping wet hair was sticking to my neck and shoulders; it made me feel as though someone was touching me. I carried on as steadily as I could.

Eventually I got to the bedroom and closed the door quietly just in case, by some stroke of luck, he hadn't heard me leaving the bathroom. As quickly as possible I got dressed, not bothering to dry myself. My overriding thought was that there was no way could I contemplate having to defend myself naked.

A few minutes passed.

My heart was thumping.

I daren't move.

Finally I allowed myself to listen.

Nothing... no sound of anyone climbing the stairs to find me, no sound of anyone walking about the house. For a while I couldn't allow myself to believe it. I thought that maybe he was already up there with me, waiting on the other side of the door, planning his entrance. I just had to sit it out. Still nothing. I wondered if I should turn on the radio; that would take my mind off things. I decided against it. I waited, struggling to keep my breathing calm and regular.

Time passed. I have no idea how much time. I stayed in the room, motionless, until my boyfriend got back. It was overwhelming to hear him chatting with the other members of the household, coming upstairs, and to actually see him walk into the bedroom. Normality flooded back to me. I explained everything, crying but not wanting to come across as hysterical. He assured me that he found the back and front doors locked when he arrived and there were no obvious signs of anything being out of place downstairs.

I asked him loads of questions; getting him to verify where things were, if internal doors were shut, if there was anything that could have possibly been moved, or could have been the cause of the footsteps I heard. To him, nothing had changed since they left to play squash a few hours earlier.

I don't usually speak about this type of event. I am not someone who is particularly 'sensitive' to paranormal events or strange atmospheres. However, I have occasionally witnessed phenomena that I can find no explanation for. The most important thing for me after this ordeal was that I was believed.

That 'person' downstairs was not an intruder, not a thief. It was 'someone' who knew the layout of the house and was walking around, going about their daily life.

My boyfriend was concerned for me, but not at all surprised by my account of what happened. He merely added it into his repertoire of tales about the house. You see, I discovered that this was just one of many true stories about inexplicable things that had gone on there over the years. Inexplicable to us in our everyday world, but not so if you believe in the continuous bond between buildings and their former inhabitants.

The Boy And The Ball

Kevin A

When I was a lad in the late sixties, I stayed in a place near Liverpool called Thornton. It was full of 'thirties houses and new developments. My house was one that was built around the end of the Second World War, so it wasn't that old when I was there. It seemed new to me. Looking back, all the windows were proper and the floors were polished. Hardly any signs of scuff marks.

I was an only child, my dad worked for the government and my mum worked in a local sweet shop part-time. I loved reading books from a very young age, and so I was never lonely. If I knew Mum had to go and work after school, I'd pick a book and get stuck in. My favourites were adventures like Journey To The Centre Of The Earth by Jules Verne. I had quite the imagination!

I think that's the reason why my parents didn't believe me when I told them about 'the boy'.

It started in the summer, in the daytime. My bedroom was on the ground floor by a room we called the laundry room, where there was a big twin tub and a mangle. Dad also kept his tools in there and some other bits and pieces. Near my bedroom and the laundry room was a back door leading to our garden. It was a simple garden, just a square lawn with a flower border on three sides.

On this particular day Dad was at home. He was in the kitchen reading a newspaper and Mum was doing an extra shift at the shop. I was about eight years old. I was lying on my bed reading a book and I heard a noise in the hallway by my door. I assumed it was my dad walking past on his way from the kitchen to the back door. Then a minute or so later I heard it again, except this time something hit the bottom of my closed bedroom door.

I got up to see what it was, and to my surprise it was a rubber ball; about the size of a tennis ball, but solid rubber and blue. I didn't recognise it as one of my own toys, so I rolled it along towards the laundry room and got back to reading my book.

Then there were the noises again.

There was a sound of walking then a thud. Something thumped my door. I got up to find out what was going on. It was the same blue ball. I wasn't really thinking or caring where it had come from; I was only a kid. So I threw it out of the back door this time, into the garden, and got back to reading. Slightly irritated by the second interruption I thought nothing of it, and a few days went by without incident.

Then one overcast day the same thing happened; some shuffling noises near the laundry room and a familiar thud on my door. The blue ball was lying in the middle of the hall, this time there was a shadow near the laundry room. The door was open inwards and I could see a dark shape a few feet high. It caught my eye but not enough to interest me. I was about to go back into my room and leave the ball there when a small voice whispered:

"Can I get me ball back?"

It wasn't your stereotypical 'creepy' horror movie voice. It just sounded like a little kid, maybe a five year old. Like I said, I was a kid too and so I did what it asked. I rolled the ball in the general direction and didn't ask any questions.

The voice said 'thank you' and I went back to my room. I was trying to get back into my book, but something was niggling me. I couldn't get comfortable, and I was a bit intrigued about this little child being inside our house. I got up and went to the hallway. There was no 'shadow' by the laundry room anymore, and no sign of the ball.

That evening I asked my parents about the neighbours. I asked if they had children, I asked what they did for a job, all sorts of questions. My mum was happy to indulge me, and my dad was less forthcoming. After a while he told me to simmer down and eat the rest of my dinner so he could have some peace. According to my mum, neither of the houses either side of us had small children living there - so that ruled out a theory I had been hatching, that the child climbed over our fence to get his ball both times and had let himself in.

The next day I had to go with my mum to see one of her friends who lived two streets away. The houses backed onto ours with an overgrown alley between them. Her friend didn't have any kids so I brought a book with me and a comic. It was sunny and I sat on the back steps of their house reading. I was actually having a great time, the concrete was warm under my legs; I remember being really relaxed. It sticks in my head to this day, just a feeling of a perfect summer afternoon... then I heard footsteps, kind of shuffling along the end of the garden path.

Their garden was quite a good length and backed onto the alley, at the opposite end, about thirty houses down from our own back gate. Mum and her friend were inside in the dining room talking away. I looked up from my book and there was a boy standing at the end of the garden, near the wooden back gate. He waved to me. He was small, about five years old.

"Hullo", he said. I waved at him, but he didn't come closer, so I got up and wandered over, leaving my book and comic on the step.

I asked him his name but he didn't tell me. He just sort of stood there, not quite looking at me. I thought this was strange but, again, I was a kid so I just took everything as it came, without question. He was wearing a grey school uniform; grey shorts, white socks, little brown shoes and a grey cap. I didn't recognise the school emblem, so I asked him. He told me it was on Addison Street, but didn't give me the name. I didn't recognise the road name so I assumed it was somewhere outside of Thornton, in the city.

We stood there awkwardly for a bit, then I offered to show him my comic. I turned around to indicate where it was on the back steps, but when I turned back he had vanished. It was reasonable for me to guess that he'd legged it over or out of the back gate into the alley. I didn't chase after him because I knew there were a load of brambles and I didn't want to get scratched up.

*　　　*　　　*

A few days passed and it was the weekend again. Mum wasn't working so Dad took us out on a drive to go and get ice creams at Crosby. We spent all day playing on the sand dunes. By the time we got home it was nearly teatime.

I had a bath and got into my smart clothes ready for the meal, Mum was in the kitchen cooking. While I was getting dressed I heard her shout my name really loudly, like she was surprised or shocked. I wasn't a cheeky lad. I didn't really give my parents any trouble, so I was confused as to why she shouted. I ran down the hallway and she was standing there with her hands on her hips looking flustered.

"Are you messin' Kevin Michael [redacted]?" She used my full name, so I must have done something wrong. She pointed at the floor under the table. There was the blue rubber ball. "I could've fallen and broken my leg! What if I was holding a boiling pan of water?" I stared blankly at her. "What have I told you about putting your toys away?"

I don't remember what I said in reply, but I do remember that I picked up the ball and went back to my room to finish getting into my clean clothes. I sat on the bed and threw the ball against the wooden headboard. It was really bouncy and I got into a good rhythm. That's when I heard the child's voice from outside the door.

"'Scuse me, can I have me ball back?"

I opened the door and there was the kid again; still in his little school uniform, looking at me as if I was only half there, kind of staring through me.

I looked at the clock in the hallway behind him. I said something like:

"It's nearly six o'clock. Won't your parents be looking for you?" The kid shook his head. "Where do you live?" The kid didn't answer. "Shall I get my dad to phone someone to pick you up?" The kid was still silent, staring at me with that odd look.

"Can I have me ball back?" he asked again. I felt cold. I turned away, took the ball off my bed to hand to him...

... It wasn't there. I turned around to speak to the kid again, and he had also gone. Vanished. I poked my head out into the hallway. The back door was shut, the front door was shut and the laundry room door was shut. The only place he could have gone was upstairs. I rushed up there so fast I tripped up, and my dad came out of his bedroom onto the landing.

"Whatever is the matter?" he asked.

I was so focussed on trying to see where the boy had gone that I didn't reply, I just pushed past him. I checked the end bedroom, my parents' bedroom, the bathroom, and the sewing room - he was nowhere to be seen!

My dad was understandably irritated and I got a clip around the ear for being a nuisance to my mum, and for barging past him. At the dinner table I tried to explain myself. I tried to explain about the small boy, and all they kept replying with was "what an imagination!" or "you're so creative lad!" In the end I gave up and just ate my meal.

The one thing I clearly remember about the whole incident was that strange school he mentioned, Addison Street. In a moment of boredom, years later, I had a look on the microfiche machines at the local library for something I was working on in my spare time. A name caught my eye. There was an article about day schools in Liverpool. Addison Street Day Industrial School was from Victorian times, a term used for what were once called poor schools.

As far as I can remember it was a sort of boarding school for children whose parents were of ill repute or had been deemed too drunk to look after children at home - so they spent their day at the school doing some lessons and some industrial crafts like mat making.

I honestly have no idea why the little boy showed up in Thornton, miles from his school. Or why he kept running off. I thought for a long time that he was not of this world, a spirit child, but I reasoned that out of myself because I am not a great believer in the supernatural realm. It's an interesting story to recount, and even now my elderly parents still think I have an overactive imagination.

Post Script

(transcribed from phone call)

Kate: Hi Kevin, I wanted to give you a ring because I did some digging about your encounter with the little boy.

Kevin: Yes?

Kate: So, you told me the address was at [redacted] in Thornton? Well, did you know about your neighbour?

Kevin: The man or the young couple?

Kate: The old man, he would have been in his seventies or older at the time you were about eight years old.

Kevin: Yes, he stayed in the house next door and his daughter came in to help him because he was quite frail. I went over with my mum a couple of times and he gave me penny sweets. We helped clear out the house after the funeral. Mr [redacted] he was called.

Kate: I actually was able to run his name through some local databases because you knew his first name and surname. I'm pretty sure that he attended Addison Street Day Industrial School.

Kevin: Really?

Kate: Yes, I had them look up the details of his admission. It turns out his mother died when he was a toddler and his dad turned to drink. He had three brothers and a sister. They all went to the school. Court ordered, a bit like social services now.

Kevin: That's quite a coincidence!

Kate: Well, it gets a bit stranger... his youngest brother was unwell, and didn't make it to adulthood. He passed away from scarlet fever when he was four and a half years old. There was apparently a note added to the entry to say that he didn't have suitable clothes to be buried in, and the matron at the school asked for donations so that he could be buried in full school uniform. What do you think about that?

Kevin: [silence] Like I say, it's a coincidence. I wonder if Mr [redacted] ever saw the boy at his house? Maybe it was his little brother's spirit coming to visit because he knew the guy was on his last legs... [silence] or what if it was him reliving his school days, like an out of body experience? The little boy was him... [laughs nervously] Oh, you've given me goosebumps! I don't really know what to say! I didn't think that far into it when it happened.

Kate: [Laughing] That's okay, I just wanted you to know what I had discovered.

Kevin: It's certainly given me some things to mull over.

I Saw Her Too

William N

When you move house everything feels weird. Being a kid doesn't take that away. Adults think kids find the moving experience 'exciting' and 'an adventure', but really they find it boring. The anxiety of a new bedroom, a new kitchen, different ways to school; it's uncomfortable.

In 1993 my family moved from a grey concrete tower block in Glasgow to a grey concrete house in Cumbernauld. As a grown up, looking back on that time I can see that it was a great opportunity, and my parents only wanted the best for me (10) and my brother (13). The schools were better, the town was only thirty years old, there were trees and grassy areas... It's just in the moment I felt my whole world collapse.

The reason they chose to relocate to Cumbernauld is that my granny and granda lived there and so did one of my cousins. It meant more babysitting options for them and, having saved a bit of money by renting in the block, it was a 'now or never' kind of thing.

After all the boxes had been thrown away or burnt the house wasn't actually half bad. We had our own bedrooms and I had made a few friends at school. I was looking forward to going to high school and my brother had a girlfriend so he wasn't around much. There was just one issue. One kind of embarrassing issue...

I'll tell you right now, I shouldn't have felt worried about talking to my parents about this, but it was the 90s and my da was one of those "no son of mine is goin' tae have feelins, that's wummin's stuff". Little did I know that they were going through the start of a long and messy divorce. I just thought the stony silence and distant stares were because they didn't want me to talk to them. There was *no way* I could have told my da about my little problem, and my ma would have got all funny about it... causing more arguments.

The 'embarrassing issue' was that I was suddenly scared of the dark. It had never bothered me running up and down the corridors of the old tower block. Even hiding out in the derelict car parks in Glasgow with my pals long past curfew - I wasn't frightened. There was just something about the stairway and the landing in this new house that... wasn't quite right.

I used to dread having to go upstairs in the gloomy autumn evenings and do my homework in my bedroom; worse still was going along the landing for a pee in the middle of the night. This went on for probably a whole year. My parents were on edge for their own reasons. I was mostly okay, but still had anxious feelings about the stairs. Then, luckily, one Saturday evening I got punched in the shoulder by my brother.

I call it lucky because without that punch I would never have started the conversation that led to us becoming closer. I would never have found out that I wasn't the only one in the house experiencing those weird sensations.

So, I was laying on my bed flicking through a Warhammer magazine and looking at models I wanted to buy with my pocket money. All of a sudden my brother (now 15) came bursting into my room with a face like thunder. He was bigger than me, muscly, erring on the side of fat. He was nearly six foot tall and I was a scrawny five foot nothing.

"You little shite! Give it back!" he shouted at me. I ignored him, because I had no idea what he was talking about. He slammed the door behind him as he walked further into my bedroom. "You think you're so fuckin' clever, just give it back an' I won't tell anyone!" I carried on looking at my magazine expecting him to storm out, but he didn't. Instead he punched down hard on my shoulder and I yelped.

"Fuck sake!" I shouted and moved backwards on the bed. He was looming over me.

"Give. It. Back. You. Wee. Prick." he said through gritted teeth. He leant down and grabbed my magazine, threatening to rip it up, dangling it in mid-air. "Tell me where it is or *this* is goin' in the bin!" I felt like I was going to cry and I remember at that point he must have realised I wasn't faking it. He looked awkward and dropped the magazine. I snatched it back, and I don't know what made me say it, but I kind of squeaked:

"Maybe the old lady took it!"

Instantly his face went white and he looked like he was going to puke. He sat on the end of my bed.

"What did you say?" I repeated myself and then I frowned. I had never thought of putting a figure or a personification to the horrible feeling I got on the stairs. As soon as the words left my mouth it sounded right.

I remembered a few times throughout the year when I had assumed my ma had got my granny in to babysit me. I had seen an old woman in a cleaning tabard, wearing a knee-length skirt, mule slippers and a pink coloured jumper... I had thought it was my granny... but thinking about it at that moment with my brother, I hadn't spoken to her and she hadn't spoken to me. She'd just been at the top of the stairs when I looked up on the way to the kitchen for a biscuit or a drink.

Why had my brain suddenly decided to attribute a figure to the uneasy feelings? Maybe I had already seen the figure and was so scared I had blanked it out. At that moment we both heard a thud noise on the landing and instead of predicting it to be our da coming up to see what all the shouting was about, we both jumped in fright! Then the strangest thing of all happened, my brother started to tell me how scared he was of the house.

You have to realise this is a macho, fifteen year old Glaswegian boy talking earnestly about scary old ladies! At first I thought it was a wind-up, but as his voice got higher and higher I realised he was being genuine. He had even forgotten about whatever it was he had lost.

"... I saw her too; the other night, there, when I was comin' in from football practise after school. It was dark already. I don't know where you were. Da was at work an' nobody else was in. Fuckin' scared me stiff!"

He described in detail that when we moved in on the first day he was pretty happy about coming to a new place because he was older and starting a new high school anyway so it made no difference to him. He liked the thought of having his own bedroom, and he already hung around with our cousin and her mates.

That first afternoon, when all the boxes had been dropped off by the two vans, he stayed in the house unpacking his belongings while we all went off to get a chippy for dinner. He had needed a pair of scissors from downstairs and when he came out onto the landing the old woman was standing there. Not like a ghost or anything; a normal, solid old woman.

"... I tried to talk to her, even asked if she knew Granny, but she didn't reply and I noticed her eyes were all messed up. I ran back in my room and hid under the duvet until you all got back. I never said anything because -" He didn't have to tell me why he didn't tell us. Da would have laughed so hard in his face that he choked. Then he'd have told all his mates, they'd tell their children and my brother would have been a laughing stock.

Something happened in that moment. We ended up talking for ages. We didn't even hear our parents calling us down for dinner. After that Saturday evening we started hanging out more, playing on our Sega Megadrive console and we never argued as much. Strangely, neither of us mentioned seeing the creepy old woman for weeks. It was nearly Christmas before things started to get weird again.

*   *   *

I was doing well at school and even though things were deteriorating between my parents, having my brother as an ally rather than an enemy was pretty cool. We had an unspoken rule that nobody outside of us two would ever know about the old woman and the uneasy feeling on the stairs. We wanted to ignore it and pretend it never happened.

There were a couple of times when I would be running upstairs to get a book or something from my room and I'd suddenly stop on the landing with the feeling of being watched - but nothing major. We did, however, annoy our parents no end by constantly leaving the main hallway and landing lights on.

There was a switch by the front door for the hall light, which illuminated the bottom half of the stairs. Then to turn on the landing light you needed to go all the way along to the bathroom at the far end, in almost darkness. We worked out, through repetition, how many steps it took from the middle of the staircase up and along the landing to the switch. So we used to bound up the stairs taking over-exaggerated leaps. Our ma was constantly shouting; "You're like a herd of bloody elephants so ye are!"

If it was night time and one of us went for a pee, we would dash along to the switch near the bathroom, turn both bulbs on, do our business then run back to our room without turning off the lights. If our parents were still awake they'd shout up "It's like fuckin' Blackpool Illuminations in here! Turn off those bloody lights! I'm not made of money!" It sounds like a parody now, but they honestly would shout things like that at least once a day... Any eighties or nineties kid in the UK can relate I'm sure!

We were really excited about Christmas. We had already experienced a family Christmas the first year of living at the house; it had been a bit of a flop. This year our ma was going down to Ayrshire to spend time with her sister and we were spending a week going to and from Granny and Granda's house with Da and our Uncle Jim. We were especially excited because Da had got a pay rise and promised to get us a bike each.

Christmas Eve came and Ma went off on the coach to her sister's. It was really wet and mild; it didn't feel much like winter let alone Christmas. My brother was in a mood, some of his friends had cancelled their plans (to go out drinking, sitting beneath one of the local bridges and making a bonfire). He was in his room sulking. The moment my ma left my da rubbed his hands together and made an over-the-top gesture of praying to God.

"Right lads! *Praise the Lord!* You're on ye own for a bit while I get oan the whiskey with *Jimmy-boy*! Aha! See ye's later!"

With that I was left sitting in the living room alone watching whatever crap was on terrestrial TV. There was a black and white film about Scrooge, then some news announcements. I remember being really, really bored. I decided to take a bath and get into my pyjamas early. After my bath I was walking to my room and I could hear Christmas music coming from my brother's room. All the lights were on, including some coloured fairy lights around the bannisters.

I stopped a while on the landing with the towel wrapped around my waist, and thought about whether I should go downstairs and make something to eat. I walked closer to the top of the stairs and I leaned on the landing bannister rail. I was just about to take my first barefoot step down the stairs when I felt a massive shove on the middle of my back!

Stumbling forward I nearly missed my footing and I immediately became angry, shouting,

"Shaun, you fuckin' idiot! I could have broken my neck!"

I turned around instantly to lash out at my brother but his door was still shut and the music was playing just as before. No footsteps, nothing to suggest he had been there behind me. In fact, a couple of seconds later he banged open his door looking worried, thinking I'd had an accident.

I told him exactly what had happened and what it felt like. He didn't dismiss it, but at the same time he wasn't convinced. He told me my back probably went into spasm from being in the hot bath too long then walking out onto the cold landing. He went back to his room, and I went to get dressed. Even though the lights were on I didn't go back out onto the landing. I can tell you now, I even peed in an empty Iron Bru bottle in my room because I was too nervous to go to the bathroom!

Christmas came and went. Da had a stinking hangover, Uncle Jim got in a fight with him about who owed who money from the drinking session on Christmas Eve. Granny threw both of them out and told them to have a square go in the street - if they wanted to act like animals they could embarrass themselves outside not at the dinner table. Ma didn't call. We didn't get our bikes. Nothing much happened.

On Boxing Day I went round to Granny's with a note from my da apologising. She gave me a cup of hot chocolate and asked me how I was liking the 'new house'. I thought it was a bit mad to call it that because we'd been living there for ages. I wondered if my brother had said something to her... She kept looking at me over the top of her coffee cup and being all evasive. So after a polite amount of time I left with a load of turkey sandwiches and Christmas fruitcake wrapped in foil to 'tide us over' until Ma came home.

*   *   *

About a week after Christmas things went back to normal. School wasn't open yet but my parents were at work as if the festive period had never even happened. The weather was dreich, my brother in a dark mood, and I spent hours mastering the few Megadrive games we had played countless times.

I had the sound turned down low on my TV so I could barely hear the jumping and hitting sound effects on the game. I had heard the music so often it started to become a pain. I remember that I was about to give up and ask my brother if he wanted a snack, when I heard the most almighty clatter on the stairs and a scream!

I jumped up and went onto the landing. I couldn't see what had happened at first, then I saw Shaun knocked out cold at the bottom of the stairs! For a moment I thought he was dead... then he opened his eyes and started screaming;

"My leg! My leg! My fuckin' leg's broke! Oh man! Fuck 'sake man! Call the ambulance!"

I ran downstairs and used the landline to call 999, it all happened so quickly. They arrived before Ma or Da could. My parents were working and they didn't have a car, they had to get buses back from Falkirk and Airdrie.

When they did arrive they told me to grab my brother's clothes from his room and some books and put them in his gym bag. Then, without even stopping to ask me, they snatched the bag and ran off to the local bus stop to catch a ride into Glasgow to see my brother at The Royal Infirmary. And that was that.

I was left in the house with just the landline phone, the TV and myself.

I thought about going up to visit my granny but I didn't know where the spare house keys were to lock up the back door.

*   *   *

My brother came home from the hospital two days later. He had a full cast right up to his hip on his left leg. He also had bruised ribs and a chipped tooth. He was so out of it on painkillers that he kept repeating to anyone that would listen, "she pushed me... she pushed me... the crazy bitch..." Of course people humoured him, but when we were alone I was freaking out.

He looked at me with glassy drugged-up eyes and told me that he thought he'd heard a noise on the landing. When he saw nobody was there he decided to go downstairs and watch TV. While he was making that decision he'd felt a gust of cold air go past him, then he felt like he was being strangled. When he tried to call out for me he felt the sensation of being pushed down the stairs with a hard shove.

More than that, when he opened his eyes and saw me at the top of the stairs, the creepy vision of the old lady was standing behind me and her eyes were black. He said he was sure she was going to push me too, but when I started running she didn't move down the stairs after me. It was like she was stuck on the landing; just standing there in her tabard and 'old lady' clothes.

Because of his stookie he couldn't walk upstairs and my ma turned the dining room into a makeshift bedroom with a second-hand sofa bed and some cushions. After 'the big accident' we experienced similar situations with the Old Lady almost every week. It would come to the point sometimes when even Ma would shout down, "Has anyone seen my sweater it's Baltic up here!" And we'd look at each other knowing that it wasn't just cold, it was something more...

There's nothing much else to say apart from I moved out when I was seventeen, and I couldn't have been happier. I went to art college and got a grant so that I could live in a tiny flat in another scheme in Cumbernauld. It was utter bliss knowing that after nearly a decade of having to, literally, watch my back in my own home I could close my eyes at night and listen to the sound of the neighbourhood rather than my own heartbeat.

Many years later when my granny was ill, on her death bed so to speak, she did tell me about our old house. She said the reason it was so cheap was because in the nineteen seventies an alcoholic man and wife lived there and there was an 'accident' where the man was found at the bottom of the stairs with a broken neck. The belief was that he fell down the stairs while he was drunk, but all the neighbours knew the wife had wanted him dead for years after he cheated on her at a nightclub in town.

Apparently, after his funeral, the wife got so drunk and dour that she went to the bedroom, took a packet of pills and topped herself. Now, all this could be hear-say. My granny was a great one for local gossip, but I had also heard a rumour about this incident (not knowing it was at my home) when I was at school.

Kids at the high school used to say "Watch out for Auntie Maggie. If you say her name three times in the mirror she'll come and push you down the stairs..." And my granny did tell me the lady who lived there had been called Margaret but everyone called her Maggie.

I decided to submit this account of what happened because I have always looked back on 'the fear' and wondered if it was an overactive imagination or stress from my parents getting divorced... any number of things! There's just something about the way it felt, the *reality* of it, that I can't put down to fantasy. The first moment when my brother told me he'd seen her too was such a turning point in my life. I can't imagine what I would have felt like otherwise... Probably thinking that I was going mad, having raging teenage hormones and an imaginary evil old woman in the house!

Knowing that someone else was there with me, someone I could trust, made all the difference. I once asked my ma (when I had moved out), if she had anything weird happen in the house after we moved in there. She smiled at me and shrugged in a non-committal way, so I guess I'll never know.

The Invisible Man

Lydie D

This one time I was out with some friends for a coffee in Port Glasgow. It was getting late and so we decided to go to Lidl supermarket to do some shopping for dinner before saying goodbye. When we had finished in the store we stood around chatting in the car park, smoking cigarettes and making plans for when to meet up next.

One of my friends had a young border collie which was really well behaved. Earlier in the day, she had been showing us how many tricks it could do and such like. While we were talking, the dog kept pulling on its lead and eventually slipped its collar.

Instead of running off in the empty car park, it stopped and looked up as if someone had called its name. We all watched as it started walking slowly, like it was with someone and coming to heel.

Then the dog sat down in the middle of the car park and started raising its paw, which is a trick that we had been shown earlier. It was as if someone was telling it to do these things and it was obeying. After a couple of minutes of this show, my friend got worried and called the dog back to her.

We all saw that it started coming back, and then stopped and looked towards the thin air where it had been sitting. Then it bowed its head and came trotting back. Once she had it on the lead we all quickly said goodbye and agreed that this was a really strange thing to happen.

I'm not one to believe in the supernatural and there is probably a good explanation as to why it happened. You could say the dog was young, the dog heard something - but it was exactly as if someone was commanding it, yet there was nobody there.

Omen

Julie C

When I was at college in 2002, I had saved up enough money from my part-time job to go on my first holiday without my family. I had never been abroad before, so two of the people I saw regularly in my college classes said we should all go together, and we settled on a cheap self-catering hotel on a Greek island. Zakynthos.

I was really excited, and also nervous about the plane ride as this would be a new experience for me. When we arrived it was clear that this would *not* be the holiday of my dreams. Firstly the 'three beds' turned out to be two beds plus a cot bed on the floor - guess who got the cot.

Secondly, all the girls wanted to do was sunbathe at the hotel next to the pool. They didn't even want to go and see the baby turtles on the local beach or explore the island. In the end, I spent lonely days walking around the small black sandy bay on my own, or waiting by the pool so we could all go out to a bar in the evening and get drinks.

Being so inexperienced, I was too afraid to go far away from the girls because I didn't speak any Greek. I was relying on them to show me how to do things in a foreign country, like order food, hail a taxi etc. Well, they soon got their just desserts.

The evening before we were due to go home, I was feeling really depressed and basically wishing that I'd spent my several hundred pounds on anything other than this awful holiday. We got ready to go into the little village and find a cheap place to eat, and that's when it happened.

Our hotel was on the top of quite a steep hill that ran all the way to the beach at the bottom. We were walking down and coming towards us was a little hunched over old lady. She was wearing black clothes and a black headscarf with gold fringing; a typical YiaYia. I have to point out that my friends were stunning, blonde eighteen year olds, and I was very much the opposite; dark hair, olive skin and quite dumpy.

My friends were walking next to me chatting, as we approached the old lady she didn't move out of the way. So I moved to one side and my friends moved to the other side of the pavement to let her through. Quick as a flash she whipped out this small olive branch with loads of leaves on it.

She waved it at my two friends and basically whacked them on the arms with it shouting,

"Bad girls! Very bad girls! You not have good lives!"

While they were reeling from this shock, the old lady walked the couple of paces over to me and put the olive branch away. She took my hand between hers and looked me dead in the eyes and said,

"You are very good girl. You do great things."

I was stunned. After a few seconds she started walking up the hill again and didn't look back. Some of the other tourists were looking at us and whispering, so my friends and I went on our way and found somewhere close by to eat, anywhere we could duck into and disappear.

When we sat in the crowded restaurant they started talking. They were really spooked and one even started crying thinking that she would be cursed, or the plane home was going to crash. They asked me what she had said to me as

116

they didn't hear it. I just told them she said the same thing but didn't hit me with the branch. I didn't want another reason for them to be against me and make it a difficult time.

All that night and the next morning, before we left to go to the airport, the girls were nervous and miserable. I felt fine and I even let them use the expensive call minutes on my phone to ring people at home in the UK. They were both crying on the calls to their parents, saying that an old lady had been mean to them. It sounded so pathetic, but I do understand that they must have been scared by it. I was intrigued.

When we eventually got back to England (with no issues on the plane), our friendship dissolved... they did have a long run of extremely bad luck. One of the girls also found out she had a life-long autoimmune illness, and the other had a string of failed relationships well into her adult life... All the time, from social media updates and via mutual friends, I saw that these 'bad things' were instigated by the girls. I was glad to not be associated with them anymore.

I don't claim to have had a perfect life since then, however I can truly say that I have a really strong conscience about moral issues. It has led me to be in awkward situations where I felt like I should take the moral high-ground when others laughed at me. It has also helped me to speak out for many people that are getting bullied or treated unfairly in the workplace. It helped me with political activism and to fight injustice for animals being treated poorly in captivity... and in many other situations where I have felt an overpowering need to do 'the right thing'.

I think back to that chance encounter on the road in Greece, and I wonder if that old lady with the watery blue eyes was predicting our futures or whether she could just sense that they were vapid, narcissistic individuals. I also wonder if I was always a 'good' person or if she changed my outlook on life when she gripped my hands...

I tried to look up anything relating to thrashing people with branches or twigs, and any occult or ancient religion on the island, but I came up dry.

The Scream

Jim G

Firstly, I feel sick just thinking about this. If you search for the castle on the Internet, these days you can get a neat little return with some easy walking routes and a link to The National Trust. In the early 2000s there were a few paranormal links where people had suggested local groups in Dorset visit the site, but nothing was conclusive.

I want to tell you about a collection of times I visited the location between 1982 and the millennium. I say that I 'visited' the place, it was more like a forced activity to help me try and lose some weight and join in with traditional family excursions. They liked to ramble. It would be fair to say that, over the course of our family holidays to that area of Dorset, I must have been to Coney's Castle about thirty times, and each time there was the same atmosphere... for different reasons.

Let me describe the area for you. It's stunning. Day or night, that area of West Dorset is beautiful and well worth a visit. Looking down from the ridge a carpet of woodland and green fields stretches away from you. You have a large Iron Age hill fort at one end called Lambert's Castle, at the other end the smaller remains belong to Coney's. At the time of writing The National Trust have on their website a perfect quote to sum them up:

"The hill forts of Lambert's Castle and Coney's Castle are less than a mile apart so you can easily explore them both in a day. Each one has a different character, but both have a rich past."

We had been going to the same little cottage in a nearby village since I could remember. It was cheap, quaint and the perfect place for me and my sister to explore without getting under our parent's feet. The castles were so close that every couple of days we would walk to Lambert's and have a picnic on one of the sweltering slopes. Then, if there was time, we would walk along the ridge road to Coney's.

In case you're not aware, the hill fort 'castles' aren't buildings made of stone or brick; they're the remains of ancient strongholds on top of prominent places. The main defence for our ancestors back then were big ditches and furrows encircling the whole encampment, sometimes with wooden spikes at the bottom. In the 80s and up until the present day, these ditches are full of brambles and small trees. Still just as painful.

We all found great fun in running around the raised areas between the ditches to see how long it would take to meet the other person coming back the other way. It was essentially a ring around the entire area and there was no possibility of getting lost. You just had to watch out for tree roots and patches of stinging nettles. The views over the rest of Dorset are breathtaking, especially on a sunny day. You can sometimes even see the coast.

We loved these family walks so much that we started going to the castles after our evening meal. It was easy to see the walking trails by moonlight, and after a blisteringly hot day the ground would still be giving off heat even though the sky was black and studded with stars.

*   *   *

Everything started to change when I got 'lost' at Coney's Castle on one of these night-time adventures. It was usual that each of us walked separately alongside one of our parents, up the lane from the cottage to the top of the ridge road. We'd choose to go left or right. Left was Lambert's, right was Coney's. For some reason this time it was my sister and I that were walking together, the adults were behind us.

We knew the road to Coney's Castle so well that we decided to run ahead to the small gravel car park lay-by and wait for our parents there. Now, bear in mind this is a straight section of open road on top of the ridge, with the dark woods of the castle ahead of us. There was no way you could get lost, even if you'd never been there before. You just go straight until you hit a gravelled area at the start of the woods. We ran forward and, me being older, I sped up making good headway. I was laughing and expecting my sister to be grumpy when she turned up last.

I didn't look behind me.

All I remember is suddenly feeling extreme fear and, although I was running, the world around me kind of slowed down and I became unsure of my footing. If you have ever been exhausted or drunk, it was that feeling of moving through viscous air. Every time my feet hit the tarmac of the road I was unsure if I was going to fall over.

Naturally I slowed down. I was breathing hard and thought I might have overexerted myself because I was pretty heavy for a kid, but that didn't help. I looked around in the moonlight and I wasn't at the part of the castle with the gravel car park, I was in a bit just over to the left where one of the small ditches started.

For me to get there I would have had to run through the gravel car park *and* through the first set of trees... an extra couple of hundred of metres. I panicked at that point and ran backwards towards the road where I met my sister and my parents who were wondering where I was.

I was so shaken that I couldn't describe what had happened; all I knew was that I didn't want to 'go back over there'. We decided to continue down the road a bit more, then head right, over a stile into an open field area so we could look out over the lights of the villages towards the sea. This was still part of the castle grounds. My sister was bored and kept whining, so my parents asked me to stay back on the road with her while they went to take some photos using a tripod.

When it was just me and her on the road my blood ran cold again. I kept telling myself I was just scared from before, but then she held my hand. She hardly ever did that. She kept saying to me that 'someone was watching us'. I tried to make a joke and tell her it was a fox or a badger, but she was getting anxious. We called to our parents and eventually they came.

We both ran as fast as we could back onto the open road on the ridge and away from Coney's Castle.

*   *   *

After that, whenever we had the opportunity to go on an evening walk we always opted to go to Lambert's Castle or down to the stream at the bottom of the village. My parents didn't feel the same as us. During the day they made us walk back to Coney's, thinking that it would rekindle our confidence. It did the complete opposite.

When you're a kid, especially if you're a kid from a

large city, you don't always know what the countryside should sound like. In a town or a city you have the constant hum of cars, buses, trains, building work, human life. So when you come to the countryside and it's quiet, you kind of expect it.

A few years after the strange night-time incident, we were being 'forced' to go and take photographs at the castles again. We had analogue cameras (it was the early 90s after all), and my parents said they wanted to include our pictures in a holiday diary. We spent a couple of hours at Lambert's Castle. It was peaceful and we saw rabbits running around. There were some cows in a field on one side of the road, and no other people on the whole hill.

After a picnic we all walked towards Coney's Castle. It was just after lunch and the day was really balmy. Considering that 'coney' means rabbit we didn't see any rabbits at all, not even on the flat grassy expanses. The small wooded areas were chilly. My parents got annoyed as I constantly asked for my jumper. My sister was waiting around by the gravel car park, and my parents had gone back to the field to look over the villages and farms in the valley towards the coast.

I decided to go and look at the 'middle' of the hill fort, which is a flat area of long grass on the left side of the road. I waded out into the mass of green stalks that were waist-high, hoping to get a good photo of the meadow... but when I went to take the picture my camera jammed. It was a wind-on type, so there was a big button to take the photo - but it wouldn't press down.

I thought at first that I had forgotten to wind on the film after my last photo, but the winding mechanism was also stuck. Everything was completely jammed. I cut my losses and trudged back, the long grass making my legs itch. I reached one of the embankments at the side which was covered with the remains of the season's bluebells. I tried to take a photo of them but, again, everything was still jammed. I sat down on the dirt path and looked up at the trees.

It took a while to register what was different. I slowly realised that there were no birds; not even bird song in the distance. I was a keen bird-watcher and in the holiday cottage garden, as well as on Lambert's Castle, there were always hundreds of small birds: great tits, green finches, hedge sparrows, blackbirds... Yet here all I could hear was the breeze rustling the leaves and grass.

I stood up and walked back to the car park area where my sister was stomping around. Apparently her camera wasn't working either and it was only on photo fifteen out of a roll of twenty-four. My counter was on eleven. After a few minutes my parents came to meet us and they also sounded irritated, their cameras weren't working! My dad had a high quality SLR with a telephoto lens set, and as soon as they had walked to the edge of the field to look down over the valley everything had ceased to work.

It was at this point that we all realised something odd was happening. When I mentioned the lack of bird song (or any other animal for that matter) my dad became uncomfortable and we walked briskly away, back down to our cottage. Strangely enough, our cameras all worked once we were back on the ridge road.

*   *   *

Anyway, my parents still believed it was a good place to go

for a short walk, and so we traipsed our way back to Coney's Castle multiple times over the next decade. As my sister and I got older we were able to decline going with them (at night was the worst), yet somehow we always ended up there as a family at least once every trip. I can tell you now, when I have visited, there have been little or no birds and certainly no bigger wildlife like rabbits or foxes - despite it being the perfect habitat.

When I was about nineteen, I went on one of my last family holidays to Dorset. I was older and going to university, I loved the area but I also wanted to save up my own money and travel abroad. Being older, my sister and I made a pact that we would go to Coney's Castle alone at night on the last evening of the holiday; a kind of sibling rivalry challenge.

We kept psyching each other out on the build-up to the walk. Mum and Dad said they would come with us but wait by a field gate next to the road, leaving us to run into the woodland area on our own. I was scared, I didn't want to let my sister see or I'd never live it down. She'd be telling all my friends what an idiot I was, scared of a few dark trees.

We left the cottage together. After Mum and Dad waited by the gate I expected her to run ahead. Instead, she walked at a steady pace and I matched her steps. She was silent and I could see her jaw was tense. I really didn't want to do this so we agreed that, instead of going into the wooded area on the left of the road, we would go to the open field on the right (where my parent's cameras had jammed).

We would walk all the way to the far edge of the field and back on our own, while the other person waited on the road next to the stile. Then we'd both walk back to where our parents were waiting. No running was allowed. If you didn't touch the fence at the far edge of the field you failed the challenge.

As always up on the ridge, the moonlight was more than adequate to see the road and the worn trail through the grass of the field. We walked down the road until we got to the old wooden stile. My sister wanted to be the first to walk the gauntlet. I grudgingly agreed to stand in the shadowy road under the edge trees, waiting for my turn.

As I watched the bright white of my sister's T-shirt get smaller and smaller, I tried to squint my eyes back along the road and make out my parent's forms against the night sky. They were too far away. Again, there were no noises. I found myself straining to hear or see anything. All of a sudden I jumped in fear! I am not ashamed to say I nearly crapped myself! I heard an extremely loud scream.

It was blood curdling!

At first I thought it could have been my sister if she had fallen over the edge of the ridge in the dark. I soon realised it hadn't come from that direction. It had come from the opposite part of the castle *behind me*, in the woodland. I tried to calm down. My heart was beating in my ears and my lower back was drenched in sweat. I didn't hear the noise again. I tried to remember what it had sounded like. I reasoned with myself that it was just a fox barking. This was the middle of rural Dorset after all.

My sister seemed to take forever to come back. I was all too happy to leave her standing on the road while I took my turn and half walked, half jogged across the open field away from the woodland. I touched the slumping barbed wire fence at the far end of the field and looked across at the pinpricks of house lights dotted cross the valley. It was so peaceful. I imagined it blanketed in snow as part of some stock footage for a traditional carol concert on TV...

Now that I had calmed myself down, reasoning that the cry must have definitely come from a fox, I started to walk back casually towards the stile. Wanting to freak out my sister as much as possible I walked slower than her, like a zombie. I could see her white T shirt as a block of colour on the road by the stile. Then my blood ran cold. Behind her, something else was moving. It was a bit taller than her and appeared to be a pale brown shape. It sounds stupid now, but try to imagine a skinny grizzly bear.

Because it was dark I had no idea what it was. I started running towards her and she began taunting me saying how I failed the challenge. I just shouted at her to get back to Mum and Dad. I felt awful and as I got closer to the stile I saw the brown figure run off into the woodland through the gravel car park. I didn't have a clue what was going on, I hadn't seen the person's face. It could have been a local person up on the castle that startled the fox... to be fair, it could have been *anything.*

My sister was already running past the car park back onto the road, and I was just on her heels asking breathlessly,

"Did you see it?! It was right there!"

She was half crying and swearing at me, telling me I was an idiot for trying to frighten her. We reached the dark silhouettes of our parents and I was immediately scolded for terrorizing my sister. She turned around and pushed me and told me that if I ever did that again she'd kill me.

Years later when I asked her what had scared her - me or something else - she refused to answer. She just said,

"You *know* what it was. I don't want to talk about it".

Anyway, that night after our argument, we went to sleep and I must have had an adrenaline crash, because I passed out straight away; either that or I was just tired from exerting myself. I still wasn't the fittest person and I hardly ever ran anywhere.

I can tell you now that I had the single most terrifying dream I have ever had. I was so struck with fear that I wet the bed. I'm not kidding. I was trapped in the dream and I didn't know it wasn't real at the time. I believed it was happening to me and, when I explain it to you, you'll think it's even stranger...

In this 'dream' it was a dark cloudy night. It was cold. I was running along the ridge road towards Coney's Castle; when I mean running, I mean pounding the ground. The road was more cracked than I remember it, paler, concrete coloured. And my footsteps sounded strange.

When I looked down I was wearing red patent stiletto shoes, and I was a woman. I had slender legs and I could see I was wearing a brown tweed skirt. In the dream I knew I was a woman, I didn't feel at all like a man, not at all like myself. I knew I was female and 'James' didn't exist. The only thought in my head was pure fear and I had to get away... from something.

I was running quite well in the heels and I had a long stride. I couldn't see the fields on either side of the road; they were just a blur I was moving so fast. I didn't look back. As I pumped my arms to run faster, I realised that I was wearing a long fur coat. It was light brown and looked expensive. I ran faster and felt my breath catch in my lungs so hard I thought I was going to vomit.

I got to the place on the road where the stile and open field were to my right, and the gravel car park lay-by, and woodland was behind me to the left. But there wasn't any neat gravel laid down, it was just a muddy patch of compacted dirt. I stood for a few moments contemplating the field to the right. It was open and steep... Then I changed my mind and, God knows why, I decided to run into the centre of Coney's Castle with its rows of ditches and embankments.

Immediately I realised this was a bad decision, but I knew I couldn't turn back. I had to get distance between me and my pursuer. I was confused, the usual paths and trails weren't there, no signage from the National Trust, and everything was very overgrown. My long, heavy fur coat kept catching on the brambles and twigs as I fought my way through but it was so cold out there that I needed it on or I'd freeze in my light blouse.

I was getting tired and I found it harder to go on. With every step my stiletto heels were digging into damp mud and my heart was pounding through my chest. That's when I heard it... more crashing through the undergrowth behind me and someone else breathing heavily. A man.

I could hear him swearing under his breath and I knew he was following my obvious trail through the foliage.

I screamed so loud that my throat felt like it ripped! It wasn't even a word, a sentence, just a scream.

Then he was on me! Beating my head with his fists until I became unconscious... that's when I woke up screaming in real life.

My sister was in the twin bed next to me and she was looking at me as if I was crazy. My whole body was drenched in sweat and the mattress was soaked from where I had peed. All I could see in my mind was the brown figure behind my sister earlier in the evening, and then I felt the dreadful, real horror of being beaten to death. It didn't even factor into my brain that I was a woman in the dream until I processed it later on.

I honestly couldn't wait for it to be morning and for us to leave. If you gave me a map now I could draw you exactly where I'm sure this woman died. I even checked all missing people's records for around the 1960s (as that's what era was implanted in my head), but there was nothing that matched up. No description or photograph that fits the woman I was in the dream.

*   *   *

You've probably read all that with a pinch of salt. It could just be the hormonal dreams of a young man; a person who's already been scared of a weird place and has an overactive imagination. But, *I know* what I saw. *I know* what that place felt like. I also know that I have never experienced that feeling again, even when I've been messing around in graveyards at night, and even when my friends forced me to do an Ouija Board and a seance when I was at university.

Nothing compares to Coney's Castle.

The Bard Of Craigmillar

Michael R

Having walked from England to Scotland I was committed to spending the rest of my days hiking the wild ways and byways of this beautiful land. This was disrupted when my companion fell off the cliffs (quite dramatically) at Dunbar and broke his crown. He had to be airlifted to a hospital in Edinburgh. I was stranded. Left alone with our dogs I caught the train.

I was now obliged to be homeless on the streets of the capital for a time, rather than travelling nomadically through the wilderness as I had planned. I procured a map of the city and looked specifically for green patches - somewhere I could pitch my tent for the night.

After studying the map, a large space called Craigmillar Park seemed my best option. On the top of the hill, amongst trees and thickets, I set up my camp. There was a ruinous castle across the open field, and I decided I would take this opportunity to explore it. It was situated with a grand view over the city. By now it was evening, and I found that at night there is no way to get inside. I walked back to my camp, a little disappointed.

Every morning from then on I would take my tent down, stash it in the bushes, then head down to the city hospital to visit my injured friend. After several hours of sitting with him I would make my way back to the meadow by Craigmillar Castle, acquiring what I needed as I walked through the city. Then it was time to feed the dogs, feed myself, and read whatever book I had managed to find in the local charity shop.

Early evening I would set the tent back up, get a fire going, cook my dinner, and enjoy the exquisite summer sunsets that seem to be endemic to that part of Scotland. During these evening rituals I became quite curious about the gatekeeper, the security guard, of the castle. He would let himself into the building and play acoustic music on an instrument that sounded like a lyre. I imagined him to be a bit of a hippy, probably on the Edinburgh folk scene, playing music in the pubs then coming straight to work.

Sometimes he would bring his friends to the castle after hours, and I would hear other acoustic instruments such as a bodhran drum, and whistles. They could get quite loud; men and women chatting, laughing and music being played on and off. It would occasionally keep me awake as I was already alert, listening out for anyone coming into the park who might cause me trouble.

After a couple of weeks of this I mentioned it in passing to my friend in hospital. I said that I couldn't believe the gatekeeper was getting away with visiting after hours, what with all the security cameras inside. I didn't expand on the subject; it was just a fleeting aside during our normal conversation.

The nightly noise continued from the castle, sometimes loud and boisterous, sometimes quiet. The guard seemed to be the only occupant wandering the top rooms (which were exposed as they had no roof).

A few days later I was visiting my friend again, and he said he had got chatting with one of the hospital cleaners, a local man who was a fountain of knowledge. The cleaner started telling my friend about the castle and so he passed on my experience of the security guard who liked to do his rounds with friends. Apparently the cleaner looked confused and said that it couldn't be true.

To his knowledge the head of security was a very strict and serious man, no one got into the castle after it closed at about five in the afternoon. Once it was locked, it was locked for good until the next morning. However, the cleaner did say there was a legend of a druid who used to live under the castle in a chamber. He had been employed as a bard for the lords and ladies when they attended gatherings. I hadn't told my friend about the music coming from the castle. The cleaner was the one that mentioned it when they were gossiping.

What does flummox me is that the cleaner, and a few other locals we spoke to in charity shops, said that people only ever saw the druid entering the castle on his own and even then that was very rare... If the spirit of the druid still abides there, what of the other people I saw and heard?

Number 30

Collaboration between:

Della H, Cath F, Trish S, Paul T and Tim G

We would like to give some context to what happened between the years of 2001 and 2011. We are not friends, and this is not a fictional collaboration. Some of us believe in spiritual entities, some of us are logic-based and believe in science. All of us were affected in different ways by this one building.

The house is on one of the oldest streets in Brighton, East Sussex. However it is not one of the oldest houses on the street. It is in a terraced row and three floors high, the top floor being in the eaves. There is another flat at the back of the property which is two storeys high, but we were unable to get hold of the residents who lived there at this time for their input.

Please bear in mind that people still live in this converted house. If you are aware of the location, be respectful if you choose to visit it.

Ground Floor Flat

Cath F

I am quite an open person; I like to think I've explored all the major religions. I do sometimes get a 'sense' of a place when I walk in, but at Number 30 - I got nothing. It all seemed (like most rented properties) quite clinical and neutral. My mind was on getting a home set up in this small studio flat, and the first few months of living with my boyfriend. Thinking of spooky stories was the last thing on my mind.

When we moved into the place we didn't have any pets, as there was a strict policy in our tenancy. But because I had been with the landlord in two previous properties they were lenient and said I could have one cat or one dog. I chose to have a dog, a rescue greyhound.

As part of the rescue process we were given background information on the dog and on-going support. This included being told that, while the dog had been racing, its former owners had given it amphetamines and other substances which caused it to be traumatised. So any weird behaviour that happened, we put it down to this.

The dog would whimper and cower into a corner of the room when we were watching TV. He refused to go upstairs to the second floor landing of the flats when we chatted to our neighbours, or gave him free rein to wander around. Basically he was a shivering wreck. We had good dog skills and knew not to feed into the behaviour. We also took him on pack walks with other dogs and greyhounds. We even contacted the rescue centre and they suggested that he 'live out his life on a duvet under the stairs, he'll be happy that way'.

After several more months of odd behaviour, we realised that this was just his demeanour and we'd have to get used to it. He was a placid dog and didn't bark or bite, but he was not really a 'dog'. He seemed like a person who had PTSD. We were then contacted by the rescue centre to see if we could look after one of his kennel mates temporarily, as this might also help to bring him out of his shell. She arrived and was the complete opposite, a great ball of energy and fun - her tail never stopped wagging.

Except in certain places.

The dogs got on really well, but our original boy didn't change. He followed his friend around, docile and with his head bowed, while she jumped and bucked and generally caused havoc... It was then that we started to notice a pattern. If my boyfriend took our dog out and I was alone in the flat, the new girl would be playing, or sleeping then, all of a sudden, she would run to a corner and start growling or baring her teeth.

I would reprimand her, but she was desperate to snarl at whatever it was in the corner. I assumed she was seeing things, as greyhounds are known to pick up on flecks of light or reflections and become fixated. She only ever stopped the behaviour when I went over and tapped her bum, telling her to go to bed - which she did reluctantly. The corner was the same place that our dog always whimpered in.

The next issue was that she also wouldn't go upstairs. She was so happy and chilled out all the time, but the moment me or my neighbours encouraged her to have a 'run around' in the main stairwell, she went it circles at the bottom of the stairs and sometimes even whimpered.

Now, these stairs were just like those in any other

internal stairwell of a normal town house. They were carpeted, there was a wooden bannister. The only difference between a normal house and the flats was that the internal doors had their own locks. It was just like a student house or shared house in every other way. It wasn't at all like a tower block or purpose built apartment complex.

In any other house I visited, the foster dog would bound up the stairs and play fetch with her ball; up and down, up and down, like a maniac. Yet at my house, she never set a foot upstairs. The same thing happened with our neighbour's spaniel. They lived at the back of the building in the old servant's annexe, and they had access to the garden. Their dog was used to stairs, but when he came into the hallway to play with my dogs... he always avoided going upstairs.

I started to think this was strange. The people on the second floor were lovely. One was a teacher and the other was an insurance broker, and when they moved out the next couple were equally as nice. The top floor was a different matter, which I'll let Tim explain in his own words. There was just no reason that the dogs should feel deterred from walking around freely up there.

Anyway, a few months after that, we gave the female dog back to the rescue centre as they had found a permanent home for her. We were struggling with our own dog because he seemed to be getting more and more withdrawn and having more and more 'episodes' where he would look into space and be 'frightened'. At points he refused to come in via the front door of the building to the hallway with the stairwell, but he was fine to come in the back way through our neighbour's flat.

All of this took its toll on us and our relationship as a

couple. We decided we couldn't cope with such a big erratic dog in our tiny flat. We just weren't a good fit, and it broke my heart to re-home him with one of my family members. As you'll be aware, it takes a while for a dog to settle in at a new place and we felt that giving him over a year with constant assistance and support we had done our best. After just a couple of days at the new household it was as if a miracle had happened!

He was running around like a puppy, sniffing at things, totally comfortable and had even started being 'naughty' and chewing up shoes and hairbrushes. You could put this down to the fact that he just didn't get on with us, or the dozens of people and dogs he met on daily walks, or his previous kennel mate, or he suddenly snapped out of his PTSD fear...

Fast forward a year or so more, and he comes to visit my flat. Everything is calm, nothing has changed from when he used to live with us. He did the exact same thing. A slight whimper at the door, and then once he was in the flat he wouldn't settle and kept whining, facing the one particular corner. The family member wasn't aware that this was one of his traits from before. They tried to get him to sit down, and even offered a space on the sofa, but he was fixated with that corner.

The last thing I want to say, is that I didn't feel scared or spooked (at that time) by the dog's behaviour. There were also no rats or pests in the walls of the house - we had the landlord check that out previously as well. I thought it was interesting, and I didn't make much of it. The last enduring memory of that flat I have though, is something that I wish I could forget.

One of my friends was sleeping over while my

boyfriend was in London for the night seeing a band gig at Brixton Academy. We had planned a night of playing video games and getting drunk. She came over and the whole mood was a little 'off'. I couldn't put my finger on it. I just knew it wasn't going to be a good evening. She ended up opening her heart to me that she was having issues with her partner, and we had the TV on in the background playing a music channel while we had a couple of glasses of wine.

It got to about midnight and the wine wasn't settling well, I thought I was going to be sick. At the same time she said she was desperate for the bathroom too. We only had one toilet in the flat. I suggested that she took my main door keys and used the communal cubicle half way up the stairs to the second floor, while I used my toilet (as I didn't want my neighbours hearing me throw up, especially late at night).

I remember not being drunk. We'd only had half a bottle of wine each over several hours and we had eaten some home-cooked pizza. She took the keys and dashed upstairs. I could hear her footsteps. I went to my bathroom and knelt down, hugging the toilet, wondering if I was going to be sick.

A few minutes later she hadn't returned to the flat. I was feeling a little less nauseous. I decided to go and see if she was alright, so I put the safety latch on my front door and walked into the hallway. There was security lighting in the hallway. You pushed a button on the wall and the light stayed on for a couple of minutes to allow you to get to where you needed to go.

I pushed the button and I saw something. It was on the mini landing between the first and second floor, outside the communal toilet... and I can't explain it even now. It was an absence of light in the shape of a man. It was quite tall and it was sort of hunched over as though it was listening at the toilet door.

When I turned the light on it 'looked' at me and I saw two glowing red eyes, and I panicked. I went straight back into my flat and made sure all my lights and lamps were turned on. I turned the music on the TV up louder so I could feel 'safe'. I was really worried about my friend, but this was in a time before smart mobile phones. She had left her mobile on my sofa and just gone to the toilet thinking she would be back soon.

A few minutes later I hear footsteps flying down the stairs at great speed, and then my friend burst into the room looking flustered. She told me that she thought one of my neighbours was being a pervert and trying to watch her pee. She said he kept rattling the door handle. She was about to call out angrily but the door opened of its own accord and, although the main light was on in the hallway, nobody was on the second floor, or the ground floor (as she could see both clearly from the landing).

After that fright she went home and refused to stay the night. I didn't tell her what I had seen, because what had I *actually* seen?

It could have been an hallucination due to the wine and feeling ill. It could have been a trick of the light when I suddenly illuminated the narrow hallway and stairs. It played on my mind quite a bit. Eventually my boyfriend and I decided to move out of the building, even though the rent was reasonable and the home-move cost us a lot of money. I just couldn't feel relaxed there anymore.

Ground Floor Flat

Paul T

I used to date a girl called Cathy. We moved in together and the relationship lasted for a few years. Some weird shit happened when I lived in Brighton. I hate to admit it, I can't work this out. So I guess there could be something paranormal about those flats, but I'm not about to start phoning Ghost Adventures or Netflix for a series.

After we lived in the converted house for a couple of years I was getting sick of my girlfriend going on about the dogs acting weird, and this one time she saw a shadow figure on the stairs. We had got chatting to our neighbours on the second floor (not about the ghost stuff) and one night they invited us up for some snacks and drinks.

On the night itself, the guy had to work as someone called in sick. He was a security guard for an agency. So it was just me, my girlfriend Cathy and our neighbour Trish. I was getting bored because they kept joking around and watching crap on the satellite TV like 'America's Next Top Model'. I heard a noise on the landing outside the flat. Trish heard it too and opened the door thinking it was her boyfriend home early. There was nobody there.

This got her talking about all the times things like that happened, and I said it was because it was a multiple occupancy building. I had lived in flats all my life and you always heard the neighbours walking around. Trish kept saying she had been having 'visions' about this man... she was acting really strangely and the mood changed to become a bit more serious.

My girlfriend got serious too and decided to tell Trish about the 'shadow man' and the dogs being weirdos, and some other little things that had happened. At this point I was ready to go back down to our flat and play my Xbox, but the girls were so insistent that they were experiencing similar things that I wanted to expose their bullshit. They weren't friends; this was the first time we had met up socially. I thought, 'If I can prove there's nothing weird Cathy will feel better and I won't have to put up with all this rubbish.'

Trish was the kind of person who worked in an office and wasn't really someone I'd choose to hang out with. It did make me feel a bit uneasy that she was into this mystic crap as she didn't have any crystals or anything around the flat. Anyway, I asked Trish to get some paper for each of them and a pen. I said they should sit as far away as possible, so Trish moved off the sofa and sat next to me at the dining table.

They were at different ends of the big room and there was no way they could see each other's answers. I made up some questions on the spot like "What is the man's name?" and "What does he do for a job?" and "What does he look like?" All the time the TV is just on some mindless channel in the background.

So they finish each question in silence and at the end I got them to hand me their papers, and I swear down, the answers were almost identical; like the name, the clothes, the profession. I got angry because I thought they had pre-planned this or spoken to each other, but Trish started to get teary when I showed her the answers on both bits of paper, and it seemed pretty genuine.

Cathy wasn't her usual outspoken self. If this was a board game or a debate she'd usually be really animated and over the top, instead she just said something like "Okay. That settles it." I still don't know if that was a set-up, and I never experienced anything myself. I don't even believe in the paranormal, but that is the closest I ever got to having an experience that I can't explain, and it was pretty trippy.

Second Floor Flat

Trish S

I'm not going to pretend that I know anything about ghosts or that stuff. I don't even watch scary movies. When I lived at number thirty I had some odd things happen that I haven't ever had before or since.

It started off with small stuff, like I'd put my earrings down on the dressing table and turn back, they would be gone. We didn't have any pets that could have knocked them off or stolen them, and the whole floor is carpeted, so they couldn't have fallen down between the boards. I never saw them again.

Then stuff started happening when my boyfriend Peter went to work. I'd think he was calling my name while I was in the kitchen. I'd come back into the living space and nobody was there and the door was still double locked. I put this down to living in a converted house with thin walls. It could have been my neighbour's TV or people walking by on the street.

I started leaving the TV on when I was home, just so there were definite voices in the room that I could pinpoint. I didn't feel scared or anything, and I really loved that flat. I worked at a dentist's as a receptionist and my boyfriend was a security guard. His shifts were all over the place but I had a nice ten 'til five set-up.

I didn't have any worries on my mind or family drama happening, I was in my mid-twenties and saving up to get married and to buy a flat of our own. I honestly had no responsibilities and nothing that was stressing me out. Then the nightmares started.

The flat was a studio style, so it had a main living area with bed, table and sofas, then a separate little shower room and toilet, and a small galley kitchen. It was the whole second floor of what once had been an old house. I say old, but it was maybe a century old, not like hundreds and hundreds of years old.

These nightmares would be about a man in a long coat who lived in the house when it was a complete house, not like it was today. The rooms were empty and dusty and he would come in with a briefcase, and there were no main lights. He would start rummaging through stuff on the ground floor, moving tables and chairs, and then he would spot me and I'd have to run upstairs to where my current flat was.

In the dream I always felt panicked and it was as if I knew he was just an evil person, a bit like how you know on a TV show or a movie when there's a bad guy. I'd be backed into a corner and this man would be coming towards me and his eyes would be glowing, like they looked the same as human eyes but they were alight.

I always woke up covered in sweat and my boyfriend would tell me to go back to sleep. I wasn't really the kind of person to tell my friends about my dreams. It was private to me and I was worried they would just laugh and not take it seriously. I didn't know my neighbours very well, sometimes I spoke to the couple downstairs in flat one, but only to play with their dog a bit and pass the time of day. The flat above me on the third floor had been empty for a long period of time.

Peter was getting a bit worried about my sleep pattern and said that we should get to know the neighbours more, and that might help me feel more calm in the flat. We invited them up for a chilled-out night and a few drinks, but on the day Peter got called in to work a night shift at the bank.

The couple were nice, in their twenties too, and we got chatting about work and the usual stuff. The man, Paul, didn't seem too sociable so I just chatted with Cath and things were going well. After an hour or so I thought I heard Peter coming up the stairs and knocking on the door so I went to open it. But nobody was there.

I started to get a bit flustered and ended up speaking briefly about odd things going on in the flat. That's when Cath said she'd noticed a few things, and then - the worst thing she could have said - she told me about a shadow figure with glowing eyes. I didn't want to let on I was terrified so I just played it off, but her boyfriend seemed really angry for some reason.

He said we should test each other and see if we come up with the same answers because, in his words, 'this bullshit' was ridiculous. I decided if I had proof I could talk to Peter and I wouldn't sound so crazy. So I tore out some paper from an old note book and I went to sit near Paul at the dining table. Cath was on the couch at the far end of the room, by the TV.

The first thing he asked was about the man's name. I

wrote down Edward. I couldn't think of a surname, but I just knew the person from my dream was called Edward. Paul asked us what he wore in our 'visions'. I wrote down it was a long, light brown trench coat, a plain grey suit, polished black shoes, trilby style hat and he carried a briefcase. Then we had to say what this man did as a job. I wrote down policeman/ detective/ something to do with investigating.

Finally he asked for his age and what time period he lived in. I wrote down he was in his late thirties or early forties, and the time period was 1920s or 1930s; before the Second World War. During this time we were both silent and we couldn't see what each other was writing. You have to remember that the only thing Cath had told me was that she thought she'd seen a shadowy figure one time, and that her dogs acted a bit weird.

We gave our bits of paper to Paul, and you should have seen his face! He went pale and then read them about three times. He flung them on the table and said something like "That doesn't prove anything". So I grabbed them and, sure enough, our answers were almost identical. I'll never forget it. It was bizarre!

I had written Edward, and so had she. I had written about a trench coat and so had she, even saying it was light brown or beige. She had also written about the suit and the trilby hat. Everything matched up except that for the job. Cath had written it was definitely a police detective, where I had just written a couple of suggestions. She had said the time period was late twenties and also that this 'Edward' was 'about ten years older than us', making him around thirty-five.

I was stunned. I had never ever thought about coincidences or spooky stuff and, after a month of having bad dreams about this man, I couldn't believe what I was reading.

The night ended after that as we were all a bit weirded out. Then a few months later Cath and Paul decided to move to a different part of the town.

Peter and me stayed in the second floor flat for about another year. This is when we got to meet Tim and his wife, who moved into the top flat. I tried to forget about the strange atmosphere, but I kept having nightmares. Eventually Peter got taken on permanently in his security job and we moved to the next town over so he could be closer to work.

I haven't had a bad dream since, even running up to my wedding with all the stress, and even when I had crazy baby brain when I was pregnant... not one bad or scary dream. I also never got my earrings back from the flat. When we moved out I checked under all the carpets but there was nothing. The same with some other small belongings, I just think there was something 'not quite right' about the whole place.

Third Floor Flat

Tim G

(transcribed)

Hi I'm Tim, I'm a plumber. I thought I'd join in with this collection because I was actually older than the other people who lived there. I had a bit more life experience, but I still get the chills whenever I think about that horrid house.

I never owned my own property, I'm self-employed and I didn't get regular money. I thought it was better to rent in case I ever needed help off the government for council tax or housing benefit if my work dried up. I had a long-term partner, but she died when I was in my thirties. I was single after that for ages and I didn't have any children. It was just me in several flats across the years; making a living, getting by.

When I was forty-nine one of my mates, as a joke, said I should go to Thailand and get a mail-order bride. He kept saying I couldn't be fifty and single, living in a bad area of town, so I kind of went along with his idea. I was well nervous, but I met a lady online and she was the same age as me.

She had one grown up daughter who was a hostess for Air Asia, and lived with her husband out there. The lady I met had left her profile on the foreign dating website but she actually already lived in England, and was employed in a beauty spa in Portsmouth. She only went back to Thailand to see her elderly parents and her daughter's family. She wanted to meet a man from the UK to settle down with.

We met up a few times at a bar in Portsmouth and I could tell she was the real deal. She wasn't one of these money-grabbing women you hear about on the TV.

She had her own job, she paid tax, and her daughter was married and working in Thailand. A couple of years later, after lots of dates and planning, we got married and she got a job in Brighton at a supermarket so we could be closer to things up this way, like London, Hastings and all that.

Her English was quite good and we didn't have trouble talking to each other, but where I was living - on a council estate - a lot of the people thought I had gone and paid for someone to come over from Thailand and marry me. It got nasty and they were being racist, we needed a new place to live.

One day I was doing a job at an estate agent's shop in town and they were making jokes about a flat they couldn't let out. They kept saying how the longest a couple was in there for was five years, then after that people stayed one or two months and handed in their tenancy without an explanation. It had been empty for nearly a year at this point and apparently the landlord was going nuts at them.

I chimed in and said I was looking for somewhere small, and asked if they could do me a deal seeing as it hadn't been let in ages. They gave me the details and said they'd speak to the landlord. I was pleased, the address was right on the seafront! Although it was a tiny attic style studio, we just needed somewhere quick to get us away from the bigots in my current block.

I got a phone call that evening saying that if I could fix the leaky shower free of charge, I could move in and get a fifty quid a month discount. This was fab. I told my wife and she was over the moon. I didn't tell her about why the flat was available. I just said I'd seen it advertised at the estate agent's.

We were able to move in a couple of weeks later, once we had the deposit sorted (which was one month's rent on top of the first month's rent). We signed a lease for eight months as a short term let. I gave them all my bank details for the standing order and, without even looking at the flat, we got the keys.

I already knew from the photos that it was your

average, plainly decorated studio flat. Everything was basic and clean, and although the ceilings were sloping we weren't that tall ourselves so we didn't really have to stoop down. It was quite nice when the sun shone in during the morning. My wife had random shift work at the supermarket, and so there were lots of times when only one of us was in the flat.

I tended to lay on the bed and watch TV or have a microwave meal, because I was tired after work. My wife liked to cook in the tiny kitchen, or do crafts like making cards and things. Because the space was so tight she had a fold-out table that she had next to the bed. She would open all the internal doors, then get the table and all her supplies out.

In the end, after a few weeks of this, I said we could take the internal doors off and stand them in the small square hallway where we kept our coats and shoes. This would make more space, and we just left the shower room door on for privacy.

That was a good set-up, the flat was airy and sun came through the kitchen window all the way to the bedroom in the afternoon too. I was really content and there was *so much* less stress than my last flat. Well, that soon changed when my wife started texting me at work.

She would send me messages like: "Tim, I'm too cold up here" or "Come home soon I'm scared". At first I just thought this was because her English wasn't her first language she was not using the words we would use, and was just missing me or lonely.

The messages started getting more extreme like "Come home now!" and "I need you home!" Whenever I called her, or came home, she would always hug me really hard and not tell me what was bothering her. After another couple of weeks of being bombarded by texts my patience was wearing thin. It was a hard day at work on this really commercial kitchen job for an awkward client. I didn't have time to reply to her phone calls. I went home and to my surprise the flat was empty. There was a note scribbled on an old envelope saying that she was in the local pub and to find her there. She'd apparently run out of phone credit and didn't want to be alone.

I thought this was *crazy*. I mean the flat was tiny, literally an attic space made into three rooms. There were lights up the stairs and no power cuts making it dark or spooky. I couldn't understand what was wrong. So, I got into some clean clothes and went to the pub where I found her sitting at a table alone, with a glass of water. She looked really out of place and straight away I could tell there was something very wrong.

She was nearly crying, and she told me that she couldn't go back to the flat because of 'the man'. I immediately thought a guy had broken in, or someone had tried to attack her, or one of the neighbours had done something... but she explained as best she could that it was the 'dark man' and he kept going between the rooms of our flat scaring her.

If I had been younger, if she had been younger, I would have thought this was a crock of rubbish. But she was mature like me, and she was very happy-go-lucky, and never made jokes about things like that. I realised that when we were at the flat she had been acting on edge and then any time we went out she was back to her normal self.

She told me it had got worse since I took the doors off, and she would be laying in bed, or cooking, and in the other room dark shadows would come out of the corner of her eyes, and sometimes she saw a man but it wasn't me... because she knew I was at work and the flat door was locked.

We still had five months left on our lease, and I was quite upset that my wife was in this much distress. I was also conflicted because I liked the flat and it was really cheap. I started to think about what the agents had been saying about the flat being empty for such long periods of time. I tried to remember if I had ever mentioned it to her, and I knew I hadn't. I didn't really know what the Thai general beliefs were on ghosts and spirits - strangely it had never come up when we were courting!

I promised that we would look for another flat as soon as possible, but we were legally bound to pay the next few months' rent here. She nodded and we went home.

I don't know if it was because of what she had told me, but when I started walking up the stairs I felt really heavy; like I was walking through a swimming pool or something. She was holding my hand really tight and hanging back a few steps so I felt like I was being dragged backwards too. I got really light-headed.

When we went in the flat I made sure all the lights were on, even in the shower room, and we could see every inch of the place. I tried to convince her everything was fine.

That night I slept on the side closest to the door to the living area, and I kept scaring myself thinking I could see things. *I knew I couldn't,* and I talked myself out of it. Any noise I heard I explained away. As a plumber I know what air in the pipes sounds like, running water in distant rooms, and fridge compressors. I could tell every little legitimate sound for what it was.

The flat didn't *feel* the same though.

In the morning I told my wife that she needed to get over this fear of being here on her own. I asked her to try really hard to come in from work, cook some food and put the TV on, or even talk to our neighbours downstairs who seemed nice. She said she would do her best.

So, I went to work. The same thing happened. When she came back from her shift and I was driving home, I got dozens of messages. "I don't want to be here!" "I'm going out until you get home!" "I hate this place!" By the time I got home and parked up I was at my wits' end. I love her very much, but this was too mental. I looked up from the inside the van to the top roof windows where our flat was. I saw my wife walking around, like a silhouette of her with the yellow main light behind her.

I didn't bother to check my phone again. I got my tool box out, and then went inside. When I got to our floor I unlocked the flat door. This was normal as we always keep it locked even though it's an internal door.

All the lights were on, but my wife was nowhere to be found.

It didn't take long to look around the tiny flat.

She was nowhere.

It sounds silly when I say it out loud, but I even looked under the bed! Nothing. I checked my phone, ready to call her, and there was a message saying that she was going to stay with her work colleague for a few days... the message had been sent over forty minutes ago.

I rang her phone and she picked up straight away. When I asked where she was she told me with her colleague 'having a coffee in Cafe Nero' in town. I could hear people talking around them so I know that's the truth. You have to understand, at this point I'm struggling to believe that I saw someone in our flat when I looked up from the street, and so I checked everything again.

The door was definitely locked, nobody came in or left the building while I was parked up outside. Nobody was in the internal stairwell when I was walking upstairs. The communal toilet by the second floor landing was open and nobody was in there. I didn't hear any doors banging or footsteps. I ruled out all the options of there being an intruder. Even our spare change was still on the bedside table.

To be honest, I was feeling a bit peaky at this point. I don't scare easily, but I was definitely a bit shaken. I texted my wife and said I wanted to stay in the flat tonight on my own and prove everything was fine. I said I'd come into her work the next day and bring her a packed lunch and we could talk about it then.

This is where it gets *mental*. Like, nobody believes me when I tell them it was just... *mental*.

I'm alone in the flat now. I cook myself some microwave noodles and I start watching a film on TV. It's some old western and it's a bit boring. Suddenly I start smelling this really bad stink. It was like I had a blocked drain and the drain was burning, like a really deep burnt gross smell. I thought I'd accidentally knocked the switch on the electric hob, and it was burning something. We often kept our bread or crisps on top of the flat hob so it had happened before that we'd melted a plastic bag or two.

I take the few steps into the kitchen but there's no burning. The smell is really bad now, like one of those glass capsule stink bombs you used to buy from a joke shop; really eggy. I go to the shower and check that nothing's blocked or backed up in the waste. It's clean, so is the toilet. I even got on my hands and knees and sniffed the shower waste pipe.

I did the same to the kitchen sink - no smell. The smell is just in the air. I go down to floor two and check with my neighbours but they can't smell anything and they haven't burned anything. I check the communal toilet, I checked with the ground floor flat and the back annexe... nobody has had an issue or burned anything.

I start going back upstairs and I get that feeling again in my whole body. It was like extreme fatigue; as if I'd been playing football all weekend and I couldn't make it up the stairs because I'm unfit. Once I was back at the top I saw I had left the door open.

I also saw somebody in the main living area of my flat.

At this moment I know there's nowhere for them to go. They're cornered and I'm right. There isn't any ghost or whatever, it's just a person except....

... There was no attic space for them to crawl into or have come out of, our flat *was* the attic.

There's no cupboard or door leading to the other houses on the street they could have used as a crawl space. The roof windows aren't big enough to get out of, and anyway, the roof is pitched really steeply. The front door to the flat is the only way out and I was standing there.

I call to the person and ask them to come to the door. I said I wasn't angry I just wanted to know what's going on. No reply. I plucked up the courage to go into the flat and

155

guess what - nobody there. The smell was still there, but fainter. I assumed it was because I left the door open. All of this was too weird. I sat down on the bed and started to watch the end of the film.

Nothing else happened and the smell went away. I was so knackered by this point that I fell asleep with the TV on and the room light on. I forgot that my wife was at her friend's and I assumed I was in bed like normal (not actually laying on top of the duvet in my clothes as I was in reality). I rolled over and nearly fell off the bed - then I smelled it again.

It was really pungent. It's one of the things you notice as a plumber. You can just tell wet, dank smells and pretty much know what's causing them. I had no idea with this one. I took my clothes off and got under the covers. I remember laying on my wife's side of the bed and just looking through the open doorway. Ahead of me was the tiny square patch of floor that was the entrance hall with our shoe rack and coats. To the right was the tiny kitchen and I could see the kitchen window and the night sky outside.

At that moment the sky got blocked out by a dark shape walking across the window, it seemed to be inside the building. Now, that's impossible because the shower room wall made the kitchen so small that you couldn't walk left to right across the window. Kitchen room is the width of one person standing still. You'd have to walk front to back and you wouldn't be able to obscure the full window. This shadow thing went left to right.

At the same time my brain was trying to deal with that, I thought I saw the cooker hob red LED lights on, like little pin pricks in the darkness. I was half out of my mind with confusion and tiredness. It took about ten seconds before I realised that it wasn't the cooker lights, the two red 'lights' were closer to the floor and sort of moving around.

I sat bolt upright [laughs nervously] I know this sounds like something from a bad horror film! I wish I could make it sound more believable [laughs again] I feel like a right idiot saying this out loud. What a mug.

Anyway, I stopped looking through to the kitchen, grabbed my clothes, my phone charger, anything I thought I'd need. Then I took my van keys, locked the flat, and spent the rest of the night sleeping in the back of the van between the tools. It was extremely uncomfortable but there was no way I was going back in the flat alone.

*   *   *

And that is the last time either of us slept at the flat. My wife stayed with her friends for the next couple of weeks, and I got a cheap blow-up mattress from Argos and slept in my van, parked on the seafront. When we finally had another flat to rent we had to go back and pack all our gear into boxes.

We were nervous about going back inside, but it was a sunny day and our downstairs neighbours were out in the little front garden, pruning some of the bushes and having a cup of tea. It only took us a few trips up and down.

The flat didn't seem as weird during the day, but there was still something I couldn't put my finger on. Like, if you asked me to draw a layout of the flat, a floor plan, I could do it... but if you wanted me to draw a floor plan of where the dark thing moved around, it was like the partition walls didn't exist.

On our final trip with our last boxes the downstairs neighbours said they were sorry to see us leave, and mentioned they hadn't seen us for a while. My wife was anxious to get in the van and drive off. I stayed to make small talk. I kind of joked; "Yeah had to make a quick getaway, what with the ghost and all that! Still got five months left to pay, bet I won't see that money again!"

Then my wife chimed in using her broken English; "Tim, they not want to hear about dark man in roof, let's just go now!" My neighbours looked like they had been slapped round the face, one of them sat on the sill of the bay window.

I just knew that *they* knew what we were talking about.

Third Floor Flat –

Final Comment

Della H

(Transcribed)

Oh wow! Now you're talking, that was a long time ago. Number thirty [redacted] in Brighton. I think we were there four or five years because I was with my ex for eight years in total, and we lived there pretty much straight away when we got together. It's all we could afford while I was at college. Then we were in the other house for about four years.

Wow... that's a long time to be in that studio flat now I think about it...

I honestly didn't know that the estate agents said we were the longest tenants. It does make sense though! That place is *shady as fuck*. I was only sixteen when I moved in there and my ex was seven years older than me. It was a weird first independent living experience that's for sure.

It was a studio flat, and I was used to only having my bedroom as a private space, so I thought it was actually quite a good size. My ex had already lived in another flat with another girlfriend and said this was too small, but the rent was extremely cheap so we just dealt with it. It was only ever meant to be temporary.

I don't know what the other guy told you. [I ask for her side of the story without giving any other information away]. The road was really nice, we were right on the seafront, there was a parky bit nearby and most of the houses on the street were full houses, not split up into flats like number thirty. It wasn't posh but it certainly wasn't rough. My parents liked the area, and they thought I'd made a good decision.

College was really tough. I was studying psychology and economics because I wanted to get into some kind of business management. It was like any teenage relationship, really passionate and fiery and we argued etcetera, but it was lots of fun too. We managed to cram loads of people into the flat for mini-parties, we had pet bearded dragons up there in a big tank... you name it, it happened up there in flat three. I must have been a nightmare neighbour! [Laughs]

Now the not-so-nice part. Because I was at college and my ex was working full time, I was always in and out of the flat at different times or alone in the dark evenings. I started to feel like something wasn't right. It probably happened about a month or so after we moved in. Just a shivery feeling when I was home alone, I put it down to not having lived away from my parents before.

I didn't know the neighbours in the rest of the house, they were all older than me, and through my years there we often saw new people move in and out. In fact we knew Cath from our social circle and so when we moved out and saw the ground floor flat was available, suggested that she move in there - we didn't think she'd have any issues on the ground floor as all the 'weird' stuff was on the top floors.

I won't go into every little detail but here's a few of the more spooky ones:

My ex-boyfriend accused me of cheating on him several times across our years there. He would say he saw me through the window with another man in the flat; what looked like another man in the main room walking past the windows while he could see me in the armchair.... I was always in the flat alone when he commented on the 'other man'.

Bits of jewellery would go missing completely or turn up in the hallway downstairs on the ground floor. It's not like I'd feel my ear and think 'oh I've lost an earring', they were body bars, pieces that screwed in or bolted into each other, or pieces that were sentimental and I didn't wear. They just stayed in a box in the flat.

Then there were the nightmares. Oh God! I kind of had forgotten that!

So, these started about a year after being in the flat. I guess I put them down to the stress of my college exams and worrying about getting my first 'real' job. It would happen about three times a week. It would be like I was coming home from a night out and in the dream I'd open the ground floor main front door to the building, push the security light... then it would turn on but go out when I was half way up the stairs [on the second floor] and I'd have to run forward in the darkness to press the next security light button, but it wouldn't work.

Then I'd run up our flight of stairs to get the front door of the flat and it would already be open. Someone was laying in our bed and it wasn't my ex-boyfriend, it was a dark mass, a sort of human shape but longer and slimmer; like it had been stretched out. Then I would look around more and see that none of the walls were in the flat. It was just an open attic with all of my furniture floating about a foot off the floor.

I probably had that dream for about two or three years, so many times. I could tell you blow for blow what happens and when. Like in 'Groundhog Day' [the film] when he knows when people are going to speak or drop something. I've got goosebumps just talking about it now. It's giving me the creeps.

There's probably a billion little things I've forgotten, but that's a taste of what it was like. Can you believe I gave up that flat to go and live around the corner for £800 *more* a month! We used up all our savings just trying to get somewhere, then we split up. Totally weird times back then.

HUNGRY FOR MORE ?

If you have a story to tell and you want to share it, what better way than to submit it for our next collection?

Everyone that contributed to the book found it a cathartic experience, and you never know how many people have witnessed the same phenomenon until you come forward... just take Coney's Castle for instance. Although submitted separately, two people have made a connection through this paranormal place.

This book is not published for profit, I felt it was important to have a platform where we could explore the stranger side of life - not motivated by money or popularity.

You can follow me on social media by searching for my name, feel free to private message me and start a conversation... you never know where it may lead.

— Kate Fromings, Editor

Printed in Great Britain
by Amazon

82455729R00099